Songs of Experience

SONGS OF EXPERIENCE

Making Your Feelings an Ally of Your Faith

Roy Clements

A Division of Baker Book House Co
Grand Rapids, Michigan 49516

Published by Baker Books
a division of Baker Book House Company
P.O. Box 6287, Grand Rapids, MI 49516-6287

First American edition 1995

First published in 1993 by Christian Focus Publications Ltd., Fearn, Ross-shire, Scotland, under the title *Songs of Experience: Midnight and Dawn through the Eyes of the Psalmists*

Printed in the United States of America

Library of Congress Cataloging-in-Publication Data

Clements, Roy.
    Songs of experience : making your feelings an ally of your faith / Roy
Clements. —1st American ed.
    p.   cm.
    ISBN 0-8010-5271-8 (pbk.)
    1. Emotions—Religious aspects—Christianity—Sermons. 2. Sermons, English.
3. Bible. O.T. Psalms—Sermons. I. Title.
BV4597.3.C54 1995
248.4—dc20   95-4939

CONTENTS

INTRODUCTION

*P*eople today are looking for experience. Rationalism, with its preoccupation with scientific knowledge, has lost its dominant hold over Western culture. Subjectivism and mysticism are everywhere gaining credibility. Thinking is giving way to feeling.

In many respects it is a necessary swing of the cultural pendulum, but it has its dangers too. For there is such a thing as objective truth, and it is impossible to live meaningfully without reference to it. Our feelings can seriously mislead us if they are not controlled by a reasoning grasp of the real world.

The psalms provide the Christian with a vital biblical model of the proper integration of heart and mind. Again and again, the psalmist confesses the intensity of his feelings and invites the reader to empathize with them. But he never surrenders to mindless emotionalism. He consciously brings his feelings within the orbit of God's revealed character and will.

In a day like ours, when the cultural tide all too easily leads us to identify emotional experience with spiritual experience, the study of the psalms is a profitable corrective. Hence the publication of this volume of expositions.

Each of the following chapters is an edited version of a sermon originally preached at Eden Chapel in Cambridge as part of normal Sunday ministry. No attempt has been made to eliminate the oral style. They were not a consecutive series, but have been compiled from sermons preached over a number of years. As a result, there is some variation of style and overlap of content. In spite of these limitations, however, it is my hope that the reader will find the material digestible and enriching. The goal of the book is to encourage us to take our feelings seriously, talk about them honestly, and relate to God intimately by means of them.

Part 1

SONGS IN
THE NIGHT

1

DELIVERANCE FROM DEPRESSION

I wonder if you would consider yourself to be temperamental? One way or another, I suppose all of us are. The ancient Greeks said it has to do with our glands. Hippocrates and Galen, whom some consider to be the founders of modern medicine, believed that there were four secretions, or "humors," that ought to be present in balanced quantities in the human body. They were unpleasantly named as blood, phlegm, yellow bile, and black bile. When one or other of these component fluids in our human physiology predominated over the others, they believed that you got what we call "temperament."

The man with too much blood, for instance, was an optimistic type, a resilient sort of fellow. We still use the word *sanguine* today, coming from the Latin word for blood. The man with too much phlegm was an unemotional, lethargic individual—*phlegmatic,* as we say. The man with too much yellow bile (or choler, to use the Greek word) had an irascible, excitable temperament—he was *choleric.* The poor fellow with too much black bile was the most unfortunate of all, because he was a gloomy, despondent sort of person, the archetypal victim of depression, or as the Greeks called black bile, *melancholia.*

It is interesting that after two and a half millennia of scientific advance, the old Greek theory still holds water to some degree. Many psychiatrists today would assert that there is a physical disposition to certain kinds of emotional maladjustment. Undoubtedly the body chemistry is more complicated than the Greeks thought; modern medics would probably talk more about hormones than humors. But it is generally accepted today that the roots of some sorts of depression are organic in origin. Some of us, it seems, are naturally more inclined to feel down in the dumps than others. Whether it is built into the "hard-wiring" of our genes, or it has been programmed into our memory banks by our upbringing, a melancholy temperament is something that some of us are stuck with—like freckles, or a stutter. We just have to learn to cope with it. That is one reason, of course, why it is so thoroughly misguided and cruel to say, as some superspiritual types do, "Oh, well, Christians should never get depressed."

Such pontificating, no doubt, comes easily to those of us who are blessed with a sanguine personality. We find it easy to look on the bright side. But we must beware of attributing our emotional equilibrium to spiritual factors. There is such a thing as natural temperament. Some Christians are melancholics just as there are non-Christian melancholics, and both have a tendency to get depressed. Indeed many of the great saints that we meet, both in the Bible and down through Christian history, have had a melancholic trait to their personalities. Take prophets like Jeremiah or Elijah; think of poets like William Cowper, who wrote many hymns that are still sung today, or even C. H. Spurgeon, the great Baptist preacher. It is no denigration of the spirituality of these men that they knew unhappy moods. On the contrary, it is a tribute to their spirituality that in spite of such emotional handicaps, they nevertheless achieved so much. I suspect some of them, in fact, would have testified that the unusual intimacy of their personal walk with God was in some measure the result of the temperament that God, in his providence, had assigned to them. Depression is not necessarily a sign of spiritual weakness. It can be an opportunity for extraordinary spiritual growth.

I doubt that there is any portion of the Bible that demonstrates that point more dramatically than Psalms 42 and 43. In spite of the fact that there is a division between these two psalms in our Bible, there is little doubt that they were originally one poem. Psalm 43 has no introductory heading like all the other psalms. In fact, as the margins of some Bibles indicate, many Hebrew manuscripts don't separate Psalm 43 from its predecessor at all; they just run one into the other. When you examine carefully the structure of their composition, you will notice that when put together, they quite obviously comprise a single hymn with three stanzas and a repeated chorus. You find the chorus repeated in verses 5 and 11 of Psalm 42 and again in verse 5 of 43. This refrain not only unites the two psalms, but also defines their central theme.

> Why are you downcast, O my soul?
> Why so disturbed within me?
> Put your hope in God,
> for I will yet praise him,
> my Savior and my God.

Here is a psalm then that was clearly written out of an experience of the most intense sadness of heart; it is a psalm composed by someone in the midst of depression. As we study it we shall see that at least in this man's experience, depression wasn't the enemy of his spirituality. Instead, in a strange, even paradoxical way, it was the catalyst of his spiritual development.

We shall put the two psalms together to try to answer the author's own questions. What were the causes and symptoms of this depression? "Why are you downcast, O my soul? Why so disturbed within me?" And then we shall examine the psalmist's response to this depression: "Put your hope in God, for I will yet praise him, my Savior and my God."

Psalm 42

[1] As the deer pants for streams of water,
    so my soul pants for you, O God.
[2] My soul thirsts for God, for the living God.
    When can I go and meet with God?
[3] My tears have been my food
    day and night,
while men say to me all day long,
    "Where is your God?"
[4] These things I remember
    as I pour out my soul:
how I used to go with the multitude,
    leading the procession to the
        house of God,
with shouts of joy and thanksgiving
    among the festive throng.

[5] Why are you downcast, O my soul?
    Why so disturbed within me?
Put your hope in God,
    for I will yet praise him,
    my Savior and [6] my God.

My soul is downcast within me;
    therefore I will remember you
from the land of Jordan,
    the heights of Hermon—from
        Mount Mizar.
[7] Deep calls to deep
    in the roar of your waterfalls;
all your waves and breakers
    have swept over me.

[8] By day the LORD directs his love,
    at night his song is with me—
    a prayer to the God of my life.

[9] I say to God my Rock,
    "Why have you forgotten me?
Why must I go about mourning,
    oppressed by the enemy?"
[10] My bones suffer mortal agony
    as my foes taunt me,
saying to me all day long,
    "Where is your God?"

[11] Why are you downcast, O my soul?
    Why so disturbed within me?
Put your hope in God,
    for I will yet praise him,
    my Savior and my God.

Psalm 43

[1] Vindicate me, O God,
    and plead my cause against an
        ungodly nation;
    rescue me from deceitful and wicked
        men.
[2] You are God my stronghold.
    Why have you rejected me?
Why must I go about mourning,
    oppressed by the enemy?
[3] Send forth your light and your truth,
    let them guide me;
let them bring me to your holy
        mountain,
    to the place where you dwell.
[4] Then will I go to the altar of God,
    to God, my joy and my delight.
I will praise you with the harp,
    O God, my God.

[5] Why are you downcast, O my soul?
    Why so disturbed within me?
Put your hope in God,
    for I will yet praise him,
    my Savior and my God.

The Causes of Depression

"Spiritual" Isolation

> As the deer pants for streams of water,
>   so my soul pants for you, O God.
> My soul thirsts for God, for the living God.
>   When can I go and meet with God? (42:1–2).

Here is a man who is depressed because he feels God is a long, long way away. He likens himself to a drought-stricken animal sniffing at the dried-up riverbeds and longing for refreshment but finding none within reach. To the psalmist, the experience of God's presence seems to be equally elusive. God has become inaccessible to him. Have you felt like that sometimes? It is not all that uncommon.

Some people might want to conclude that because of the religious nature of this man's symptoms, his depression is of a particular type, unique to the people of God—what you might call *spiritual* depression. But that could be a misleading phrase. Undoubtedly this man's depression expressed itself in the context of his religious life. That is where his despondency focused in his consciousness, with his sense of God being far away. But it would be a mistake to jump to the conclusion that the cause of his gloomy mood was necessarily spiritual in nature. While it is true that the symptoms were spiritual, I have little doubt that an unbeliever, with the same kind of temperament, put in the same sort of circumstances, would probably have felt just as emotionally devastated, even though he might have expressed his depression in a different way. There is all the difference in the world between *feeling* forsaken by God, and actually *being* forsaken by God.

When a believer is depressed, that depression almost invariably results in a sense of spiritual desertion. Prayer is difficult, if not impossible. All talk of Christian joy and peace sounds like empty platitudes; and God seems remote, more like a distant relative than a heavenly Father. But this is not because God *is* remote, but because our depression makes us feel as though he is. We human beings are psychosomatic wholes—body, mind, and spirit are all joined together in us.

15

We have already said that a disturbance in our body chemistry can affect our emotional makeup, but it goes further than that. The disturbance in our emotional makeup can disturb our spiritual awareness too. There is no way we can keep our experience of God in a little hermetically-sealed compartment, impervious to outside influences, labeled "My Spiritual Life." It doesn't work like that; it is not how we are made. If you have a migraine, you are not going to feel like shouting "Alleluia" at the top of your voice; and if you are suffering from depression, you are not going to feel close to God.

I am not saying that depression can't arise in a person's life as a direct result of spiritual factors; undoubtedly it can. If, for instance, we fall into sin and are therefore suffering the emotional consequence, that is, guilt, we may find that generating in us a most profound misery. Neither ought we to underestimate the power of demonic influence to disturb emotional equilibrium on occasions. But in nine cases out of ten, what people call "spiritual depression" is nothing other than ordinary, natural depression as it affects a spiritually-minded person. It is very important to draw that distinction between symptom and cause.

Physical Isolation

The experience of the psalmist here is a case in point. There is nothing to indicate that this man was suffering the pangs of guilt or unbelief. He was simply suffering that most ordinary of human pangs: isolation. He was physically isolated for a start:

> These things I remember
> as I pour out my soul:
> how I used to go with the multitude,
> leading the procession to the house of God,
> with shouts of joy and thanksgiving
> among the festive throng (42:4).

By the sound of it, this poet was one of the Levitical singers in the choir at the temple in Jerusalem. The high point of his life had been the great religious festivals when he would take his privileged place at the head of the congregation, leading them ceremonially in through the temple gates for their annual services of celebration.

16

But for one reason or another, he could no longer participate in those jubilant occasions. People have suggested various reasons for that. One possibility is that he may have been a Northerner—verse 6 does suggest he was very familiar with the area of Mount Hermon around the upper Jordan. And if so, he was perhaps prevented from going south to Jerusalem by the royal edict of King Jeroboam, after the schism between Israel and Judah, somewhere around 930 B.C. Perhaps a rather more likely possibility is that he was simply one of those exiles, taken off into Babylonian captivity, much later on in 587 B.C. He certainly speaks in the psalm of the oppression of the enemy and the taunts of his foes.

Whatever the precise date and circumstances may have been, one thing is clear—this fellow was homesick. He was deeply attached to Jerusalem; the place meant the world to him. Yet he was forcibly separated from it and was seriously wondering if he would ever see it again. It doesn't take much imagination to see how that might depress somebody. Don't you remember the first night you ever spent away from home? Boarding school, perhaps? Or that horrible first term at university? Those who have lived abroad may know that there is nothing necessarily infantile about such feelings. Homesickness is enough to make anybody depressed. We all need physical roots, and when they are severed, we feel disconsolate.

Social Isolation

If you look carefully, you will see that this person wasn't just physically isolated, he was socially isolated too, and that is even worse. Look at verse 3:

> My tears have been my food
> day and night,
> while men say to me all day long,
> "Where is your God?"

Whether these men he is talking about were unsympathetic fellow-Israelites or those oppressive Babylonian masters, it is clear he had no friends to confide in. His social environment was hostile and humiliating—"Where is your God?" they asked him with contempt. "You

17

claim to be a believer. Well, God's not doing much for you at the moment, is he?" And those verbal barbs went home.

It had been comparatively easy to trust God amidst the camaraderie and fellowship of that temple choir going into the house of God. But now he was on his own, without emotional support or personal encouragement from his friends. To put it bluntly, he was lonely. Loneliness can make you feel terribly sad—it is enough to make anybody feel depressed. We are social creatures, gregarious by nature, and when we are deprived of supportive relationships it really gets us down. If he had been one of those more sanguine or phlegmatic kinds of personalities, he might have coped with this stress he was under without lapsing into such a state of gloom. But my guess is that he had one of those more melancholic temperaments, which are predisposed to "the blues." When someone like that experiences this combination of homesickness and loneliness, it is bound to trigger depression of some sort.

You will by now see what I mean when I say that to call this "spiritual depression" could be misleading. Spiritual in its symptoms, yes: he felt isolated from God. But I don't think it necessarily had a spiritual cause. It wasn't sin or lack of faith or the devil which had produced this morbid mood of his. It was a perfectly natural consequence of the unfortunate situation he was in. Indeed, many of the symptoms he goes on to describe are typical of the kind of depressive reaction that anybody with a tendency to melancholia experiences in such circumstances. Anyone who has ever known a time of depression will, no doubt, find these symptoms striking a familiar chord as we enumerate them.

The Symptoms of Depression

Crying

First of all, he tells us he couldn't stop crying: "My tears have been my food day and night" (v. 3). An inability to control one's emotions is a very common feature of depression. Maybe there is just a hint, in the poetic idiom he uses to describe the habitual weeping, that in addition he had also lost his appetite. If so, that is another classic symptom of depression: "I don't feel like eating," he says. "I just feel like crying."

Fatigue

More than that, he tells us that he felt completely lacking in energy—*downcast* is the word he uses repeatedly. "My soul is downcast within me" (42:5, 11; 43:5), or literally, "My soul prostrates itself." If we were going to translate it into a contemporary idiom, we might say he felt utterly "flat." There was no spark of enthusiasm for anything, just a kind of inner fatigue, a sagging of the spirit. Depressed people often complain of being permanently tired.

Emotional Disturbance

In tension with that, he says he also felt a continual emotional upheaval going on inside him. Note that word *disturbed* that he uses repeatedly. "Why are you so disturbed within me, my soul?" (42:5, 11; 43:5). In Hebrew that word can speak of the kind of incoherent murmuring or growling of a wild animal. Maybe he is referring to the restless sighs and moans that often emerge from a depressed person. And that inner pain is even more dramatically expressed in 42:10—"My bones suffer mortal agony," or literally, "There is murder in my bones." He is saying, "I feel as if someone is sticking knives into me. My emotions are lacerated."

Feeling Overwhelmed

Then he tells us that he felt not just lacking in energy, not just emotionally disturbed, but utterly overwhelmed by things:

> Deep calls to deep
> > in the roar of your waterfalls;
> all your waves and breakers
> > have swept over me (42:7).

Deep was a word of great dread to a Jew. It was riddled with mythological associations. It did not just mean the ocean; it meant the primeval terror that had prevailed before God ordered the universe. A character in one of John Steinbeck's novels said he felt he had enough chaos inside of him for God to create a new world out of. Perhaps that is what the psalmist is saying he felt here. I don't know whether he was standing beside the mighty waterfall at Mount Hermon that he talks about in the previous verse, and was actually looking at it as he composed the psalm, or whether he was remembering it from his past. But he certainly felt some empathy with the battered rocks that lay under those turbulent cataracts. Many depressed people use similar metaphors. Often they will talk about being "drowned" by circumstances—"Everything is on top of me," they will say. Their sorrow seems to come over them repeatedly in waves, like the sea. And they will speak, as he does here, of "the deep"—some nameless dread that torments them.

Feelings of Rejection

Perhaps most characteristic of all is the language the psalmist uses to describe deprivation of affection and bereavement as in 42:9: "Why have you forgotten me?" or in 43:2: "Why have you rejected me?" And in both psalms, "I go about *mourning* because of the enemy" (42:9; 43:2). His whole personality was being torn by a sense of loss. Like a child abandoned by its mother, like a lover jilted by his fiancée, like a widow grieving for her husband, he felt bereft, devastated, heartbroken. Depression is often associated with such feelings. Nobody cares about me, he says. There was a great, aching vacuum inside his heart where that vital feeling of love and security and acceptance ought to be.

I suspect if this man had been a teenager, it might have been his relationship with his parents that became the focus of those feelings of emotional deprivation. If he were married, it might have been his wife that he felt alienated from. But this man was a believer; the dominant person in his life was not his parents or his wife. It is quite clear that the most important person in this man's life was God. And so, like a missile seeking a target, like a zoom lens focusing in on its subject, these feelings of depression that arose within him as a result of his physical and emotional isolation homed in on his relationship with God. That is where he felt it.

"As a deer pants for streams of water, so my soul pants for you, O God." For him depression became a spiritual problem and not just an emotional one. He felt spiritually depressed, but not because he was spiritually negligent in any way, but simply because he was a spiritual man. "Why are you downcast, O my soul? Why so disturbed within me?" Like so many Christians in such a situation, the inspired poet found himself bewildered and frustrated because he could perceive the incongruity, the inappropriateness of feeling like that. "I am a believer," he says. "I shouldn't feel like this. Why am I so downcast? Why so inwardly disturbed? What has happened to me? What has happened to my faith?" It is natural to ask questions like that.

Though we may think that we ought not to feel like this, there is no necessary criticism, no necessary disparagement, no necessary condemnation of our spiritual lives implicit in such an experience. Indeed, in my judgment, the very way this person wrestled with his rebel emotions, as we see him engaged in these psalms with his depression, bears testimony not to the weakness of his faith at all, but to the extraordinary vitality and tenacity of it. You don't come away from these psalms thinking to yourself, *What a spiritual wimp that fellow was!* Instead you come away just a little bit envious of him.

Response to Depression

Facing Up to Our Feelings

The first thing I want you to notice is the courageous way the psalmist faced up to his negative feelings.

> Why are you downcast, O my soul?
> Why so disturbed within me? (42:5, 11; 43:5).

Many depressed people try to find some escape from their tortured emotions—alcohol, drugs, some sort of diversion. Others erect a defensive barricade against them, trying to pretend they are OK. They go to the doctor and instead of telling the truth, namely that they feel like bursting into tears half the time, they say they've got a stomachache or back pain. They go to the pastor and instead of telling the truth and saying that they feel that God is a million miles away, they

21

confess to some minor problem of personal guidance or Bible study. Sometimes the deception is so good that the doctors and pastors are utterly fooled. Indeed, sometimes the mask is so effective that the depressed person actually believes it. It can be extraordinarily difficult to get someone to gain insight into the fact that they are depressed. But of course, neither defense nor escape tactics really help in the long run. In fact, they only make matters worse.

If we are going to cope with depression satisfactorily, we must admit our feelings, look them in the eye, and try to gain some insight into why we have them. And that is what we see the psalmist doing, first and foremost, in these psalms. It takes courage to face up to the truth like that. Many of us, especially many of us men, would have found it dented our macho image of ourselves rather too much to have to confess, "Tears have been my food day and night." But he had the courage to acknowledge his inner vulnerability. And if we are feeling depressed, that is the first thing we must do. Maybe I'm homesick; maybe I'm lonely; maybe some guilt or anxiety is eating away at me subconsciously; maybe I've lost somebody very important to me, and I haven't come to terms with my grief. Maybe I've just got a melancholy temperament and tend to get the blues now and then. Whatever the cause, there is nothing to be gained by running away from that sort of admission. We must admit our negative feelings to ourselves and also to God.

There are two splendid examples of this:

> I say to God my Rock,
>   "Why have you forgotten me?
> Why must I go about mourning,
>   oppressed by the enemy?" (42:9).

> You are God my stronghold.
>   Why have you rejected me?
> Why must I go about mourning,
>   oppressed by the enemy? (43:2).

Isn't there a note of ironic accusation in those verses? "You're supposed to be my rock, my stronghold. You are supposed to be the reliable, the immovable thing in my life. Well, the rock has moved; the stronghold has fallen; you've let me down, God. The enemy is mocking my testimony. You aren't bothered about it; you haven't done anything about it. Why?" There is indignation, perhaps an element of fury in that *Why?* And he repeats it again and again and again. Count how many times that word occurs in these two psalms.

It is a most important question to ask—not because there is any answer to it, for in 99 percent of cases there isn't one. The reason it is important to ask Why? is that in asking it we express the exasperation that is boiling away inside us. One thing psychologists observe is that very often depression is associated with feelings of repressed anger. One famous psychotherapist even called depression a state of "frozen rage." Anybody who has ever counseled a depressed person knows how often anger is there. Sometimes it may be anger associated with hurt inflicted many years earlier. Studies have shown that the loss of a parent in childhood, for instance, sometimes results in an inclination toward depression in later life. And that loss may not just be due to death; it may be due to divorce or illness or just emotional withdrawal.

Of course, when the person who is depressed is a Christian, what often happens is that those angry feelings that are bottled up within, whatever their original cause may be, get transferred to God. After all, God is our substitute parent, our Father; he is supposed to be in charge. God is our rock, our stronghold. If negative experiences come into our lives, whether as children or as adults, ultimately God is to blame. At least, so we feel. So it is far from unusual to find that a Christian suffering from depression feels inwardly angry with God, furious with him, indignant with him, exasperated with him. It is vital, if a person feels like that, to find a release valve for those feelings. We need, as we say, to get it off our chests, because if we don't, a vicious cycle of accumulating inner grievance and resentment builds up and the depression intensifies. William Blake wrote a poem that puts it very well:

> I was angry with my friend.
> I told my wrath,
> My wrath did end.
>
> I was angry with my foe.
> I told it not,
> My wrath did grow.

23

It is vital then, if we are angry with God, that we find the courage to tell him so. And that is what the psalmist is doing here. He asks, "Why?"—the implication being, "I am not pleased with you, God!"

There is a very moving incident in Peter De Vries's novel *The Blood of the Lamb* which illustrates this. The main character has a daughter who, at the crisis of the book, dies of leukemia on her twelfth birthday. The father finds himself devastated by the news, outside a church, still holding the birthday cake he had been taking to the hospital to try to bring some happiness into this special day in the girl's life. As he looks up at the crucifix on the church wall, he suddenly explodes with rage and hurls the cake at the face of Christ.

You may want to say that was an intensely blasphemous act. Perhaps it was, and yet there is a sense in which that is what Christ is on the cross for. He is a symbol of anger, the passionate anger of God against all the sin and wickedness of this world. He is the symbol of that divine anger venting itself safely, healingly. In one gigantic catharsis of divine passion God reconciles himself to a sinful world. The pain God felt on the cross was the same kind of pain that bereaved father was feeling. The evil and the injustice and the fallenness of this sick world had stolen the person he loved best. When we feel angry with God, we must remember that God is no stranger to that emotion. He doesn't mind us storming at him; he knows how much it hurts to be sinned against. He even knows what it is to feel deserted, and like the psalmist, to cry out of profound feelings of betrayal and desolation, "My God, my God, why have you forsaken me?" We must not be afraid to do the same.

Remembering the Past

The second element in the psalmist's response involves recollection. He does this in 42:4:

> These things I remember
>   as I pour out my soul:
> how I used to go with the multitude,
>   leading the procession to the house of God. . . .

My own view is that in verse 8 he is engaged in similar remembering. Although our version puts the verbs there in the present tense, they are imperfects and can just as well be interpreted in the past:

24

> By day the LORD *used to* direct his love,
>   at night his song *used to* be with me—
>   a prayer to the God of my life.

He remembers in this way because "my soul is downcast within me."

Now in one sense remembering the good old days when he had been close to God, whether through corporate worship or through his own private devotional life, may have made the psalmist feel worse. Perhaps that is what he is getting at when he says in verse 4: "I pour out my soul"—a phrase that seems to suggest that he is overcome with inner emotion as he thinks about these things. No doubt nostalgia has its negative side. Yet the way in which he moves into that chorus: "Why are you downcast, O my soul? Why so disturbed within me? Put your hope in God, for I will yet praise him, my Savior and my God," seems to suggest that this recollection of past blessing had helped him, too.

Someone has said that memories are given to us so that we can have roses in December. It is a nice thought. This man's memory enabled him to rekindle just a little of the joy that he had felt during those best of times and encouraged him to believe that he could experience such happiness again. The recollection of past blessing, for all its pathos, was a comfort to him in days of spiritual drought. It is worth nurturing memories of your good times. It is even worth writing a diary, "a diary of the soul" as some of the old Puritans used to describe it. Because when you are feeling down, reading it may just lift you up.

Speaking to Ourselves

Another thing the psalmist does, which is worth noting on a practical level, is speak to himself, as in verse 5: "Why are you downcast, O my soul? Why so disturbed within me?" Of course talking to yourself is often regarded as the first sign of lunacy; but the psalmist shows us that at least on some occasions, it is one of the finest therapies for keeping you sane. The greatest danger of depression is self-pity. It is all too easy to become preoccupied with our misery and even to start enjoying it in a kind of perverse, masochistic way. Frankly, the only route out of that kind of self-indulgence is to be a little hard on yourself. Stop allowing your feelings to dictate to you and start doing the dictating yourself.

Speak to your soul: *Soul, what are you doing feeling like this? Why are you downcast within me? Put your hope in God.* Martyn Lloyd-Jones in his book *Spiritual Depression* puts the point so well commenting on this psalm, that I really can't improve on it. He says:

> The main trouble in this whole matter of depression is that we allow ourself to talk to us, instead of talking to ourself. Take the thoughts that come to you the moment you wake up in the morning, you haven't originated them but they start talking to you and they bring back the problems of yesterday. Somebody is talking. Who is talking to you? Yourself is talking to you. Now this man's treatment was this: instead of allowing himself to talk to him, he starts talking to himself. "Why are you cast down, O my soul?" he asks. His soul had been depressing him, crushing him, so he stands up and says, Soul, listen for a moment, I will speak to you.

The main art of spiritual living, Lloyd-Jones says, is knowing how to handle yourself. You have to take yourself in hand; you have to address yourself, preach to yourself, question yourself, upbraid yourself. You must exhort yourself, "Hope thou in God," instead of muttering in this depressed and unhappy way.

Notice four things about this speaking to yourself.

Be logical. "*Why* are you downcast?" Among all the other things it does, that question exposes the irrationality of our feelings. It forces us to admit that they are out of all proportion to sound reason. So often our emotions get the better of us because we stop thinking logically.

Be realistic. The psalmist says in verse 5: "I will *yet* praise him." There was a fashion some years ago to counsel depressed people to praise God for their troubles. "Praise the Lord anyway" was the catchphrase. Well, quite frankly, at best that sort of advice is a dangerous overstatement, and at worst it is mischievous nonsense. The Bible nowhere tells us to pretend to be happy when we are not. Nothing is to be gained by being unreal about our feelings. The psalmist here looks forward to a day when he will again feel like praising God, but he doesn't force himself into some insincere and hysterical "Praise the Lord" mentality now. No, he is realistic. "I will *yet* praise him."

Be patient. "Hope in God" or as the Hebrew could equally well be translated, "Wait for God." Since depression is a phase we have to pass through, time is an indispensable part of the remedy. There are no shortcuts when we are depressed. We simply have to grit our teeth and hang in there with God until things get better. They do eventually. Faith in such circumstances is practically identical with patience.

Be firm. But supremely when you talk to yourself, be firm. Notice the uncompromising, resolute, imperative tone: "Why are you downcast, O my soul? Put your hope in God." When it comes to speaking to your soul, you can't afford to be soft on yourself.

I am not saying that anybody should ever go to a depressed person and say, "Pull yourself together." That sort of counsel doesn't help a depressed person at all. But it would be an immensely good sign if depressed persons were able to exhort themselves to pull themselves together. That would be a different thing altogether. For we are never helpless victims of our emotions. Even in our most severe depressions we still have reserves of willpower and self-control at our disposal. We can either fight our melancholy temperament or we can surrender to it. And the message of this psalmist is "Fight it." Don't collude with your melancholy. Learn to conduct an inner war with yourself, if necessary, to resist. Don't let your feelings dictate to you; you do the dictating. You be in charge.

Praying for Deliverance

The central theme of Psalm 43 is a prayer for deliverance.

> Vindicate me, O God,
>   and plead my cause against an ungodly nation;
>   rescue me from deceitful and wicked men (43:1).

In other words, "Get me out of the situation that is generating this depression, God."

> Send forth your light and your truth,
>   let them guide me;
> let them bring me to your holy mountain. . . .
> Then will I go to the altar of God,
>   to God, my joy and my delight.
> I will praise you with the harp,
>   O God, my God (43:3–4).

Of course, depressed people repeatedly say they can't pray, and often it is true. Indeed, I suspect that at the beginning of Psalm 42 the psalmist might well have been psychologically incapable of prayer. God seemed so remote to him then, it is scarcely imaginable that he would have been able meaningfully to address God. The best he can do is to talk in a detached third person fashion: "My soul thirsts . . ." not for *you,* but for *God.* His song is a morbid soliloquy.

But what makes these psalms so encouraging is that in the very act of composing his poem, this man has actually been working through his depression. And by the end of the psalm, the therapy is working. What began as a soliloquy becomes quite definitely a dialogue. Lament gives way to petition. In 42:6 he begins to use the second person: "I will remember you," he says. At first his prayer is pretty hostile as we have seen: "All your waves and breakers have swept over me" (v. 7). "I say to God my Rock, 'Why have you forgotten me?'" (v. 9).

But as his anger and his resentment are ventilated, so the depression is further lifted and more constructive types of prayer become possible. So we find in Psalm 43 this prayer for deliverance: "God, you're just; it's my circumstances that are really my problem. I am isolated, socially and physically. Deliver me then from the torture of this exile in which I am placed. God, you and I have got a personal relationship. You are my stronghold; be true to the character I know you have and guide me back home, into the experience of your grace and presence again."

Perhaps this is the most important lesson for the majority of us from these psalms. Thank God we are not all depressives. Most of us have probably never felt seriously depressed in our lives although we may have blue moods now and again. But maybe that has its unfortunate side. Maybe we would be better Christians, maybe we would be more prayerful Christians, if we did experience more negative emotions.

Note the intense longing this man felt to be close to God: "My soul thirsts for God." But the reason many of us have such shallow prayer lives is (dare I say it?) because we don't thirst for God like that. We live on meager water rations spiritually. We have just enough to keep real thirst at bay. And because we have never experienced the abject misery of total drought, we never experience the intensity of a spiritual deluge, either.

That is where the depressive has an advantage. For by temperament he can't isolate himself emotionally from God. His melancholic temperament is such that he must feel God's presence or weep for the lack of it. There are no half measures. That is why I say maybe we should envy him. Indeed, maybe we should try to empathize with his feelings more, rather than say, "Thank God, we don't feel like that."

There is a famous sermon by Paul Tillich in which he says that God is only to be truly known by people who are prepared to plumb the depths of their own human experience. Tillich is not a theologian I often agree with, but I am sure he is right about that. The one thing that disturbs me more than anything else about the kind of Christianity we see today in the twentieth century Western world is its superficiality. We just don't know the struggles of this psalmist. We are shallow Christians who have simply never met with God at this profound level of emotional engagement. We never get beyond the glib cliches, the sales talk, and the trite formulae. We have never really felt spiritually thirsty. We have never been moved profoundly about God; we have never wrestled violently with God; we have never prayed desperately to God. The whole intensity of this man's spiritual life is foreign to us. Maybe the Greeks were right: too much phlegm and not enough bile.

Don't be afraid to pray for a real experimental encounter with the living God. Don't be afraid to get beyond believing things about God, to actually sensing the living presence of God. Don't be afraid of your feelings; feelings aren't necessarily the enemy of faith. Handled rightly they are faith's great ally.

2

FACING UP TO GUILT

*S*pring, according to Tennyson, is the time when a young man's fancy lightly turns to thoughts of love. If the story of King David in the Bible is anything to go by, there may be something in that. Though, in his case, I suspect the love affair in question had more to do with the male menopause than with the spring equinox!

He was in his mid-forties when it happened, though it was springtime as well. The mid-forties are a dangerous age when a man has to face up to the fantasies that are never going to be fulfilled, the wild oats he's never going to sow. He has left the days of Romeo and Juliet behind, but he is not yet willing to be numbered with Darby and Joan. David, perhaps like many another man at that difficult mid-life period, found a vague sense of panic simmering beneath the surface of his otherwise very stable and contented existence.

It had been a hard climb to the top for him. In his youth he had spent a lot of his energy in politics; there had been wars to fight, governments to organize, things like that. But he was at the pinnacle of his power that spring day, in his mid-forties. He could afford to relax; his kingdom was secure. "What I need," he said to himself, "is a royal sabbatical. I deserve one." So he took one—you can do this if you are king. Instead of accompanying his troops on their usual springtime maneuvers, he stayed in his comfortable home in Jerusalem for a few weeks' holiday—who could blame him?

And that's when he saw her as he strolled, late one evening, around the parapets of his palace. Her name was Bathsheba, and the Bible tells us she was very beautiful. Unfortunately, she also was somebody else's wife. She was married to one of David's army officers—to be precise, Uriah the Hittite. I suppose David may have planned that it would be nothing more than a clandestine, one-night stand. After all, he was regarded as a God-fearing, morally-minded man. It is hard to believe that he would have jeopardized that reputation deliberately by playing into the hands of the court gossip-columnist. But if that was his intention, unfortunately fate was against him, for Bathsheba became pregnant. It would take more than the discretion of his personal secretary to hush that up. With Uriah, her husband, away with his regiment on border patrol, an embarrassing scandal was inevitable.

David's first thought was to cover it up. He thought of a simple plan: First, recall Uriah from duty on some feeble pretext of wanting information about how the war was going on. Second, get Uriah to sleep at home that night. Third, make sure Uriah was safely out on a campaign once again when the baby was born. Fourth, falsify the date on the birth certificate. And Bob's your uncle—or rather, David is!

But Uriah was not to be so easily duped. Perhaps he smelt a rat. It certainly irked him to be brought back from the battlefront just to answer lame enquiries from a king who really ought to have been there leading the army himself. David might have no conscience about lazing around in his cozy palace, while the young men of his nation were risking their necks for the defense of his realm, but Uriah felt differently about it. There was no way he was going to enjoy a night with his wife while his comrades-in-arms were facing the rigors of the open country. "I'll sleep in the servants' quarters," he said. For three days and three nights David wined and dined him, but to no avail. Uriah was just infuriatingly noble.

Psalm 51

[1]Have mercy on me, O God,
  according to your unfailing love;
according to your great compassion
  blot out my transgressions.
[2]Wash away all my iniquity
  and cleanse me from my sin.

[3]For I know my transgressions,
  and my sin is always before me.
[4]Against you, you only, have I sinned
  and done what is evil in your sight,
so that you are proved right when you
    speak
  and justified when you judge.
[5]Surely I was sinful at birth,
  sinful from the time my mother con-
    ceived me.
[6]Surely you desire truth in the inner parts;
  you teach me wisdom in the inmost
    place.

[7]Cleanse me with hyssop, and I will be
    clean;
  wash me, and I will be whiter than
    snow.
[8]Let me hear joy and gladness;
  let the bones you have crushed rejoice.
[9]Hide your face from my sins
  and blot out all my iniquity.

[10]Create in me a pure heart, O God,
  and renew a steadfast spirit within me.
[11]Do not cast me from your presence
  or take your Holy Spirit from me.
[12]Restore to me the joy of your salvation
  and grant me a willing spirit, to sustain
    me.

[13]Then I will teach transgressors your
    ways,
  and sinners will turn back to you.
[14]Save me from bloodguilt, O God,
  the God who saves me,
  and my tongue will sing of your
    righteousness.
[15]O Lord, open my lips,
  and my mouth will declare your praise.
[16]You do not delight in sacrifice, or I
    would bring it;
  you do not take pleasure in burnt
    offerings.
[17]The sacrifices of God are a broken spirit;
  a broken and contrite heart,
  O God, you will not despise.

[18]In your good pleasure make Zion
    prosper;
  build up the walls of Jerusalem.
[19]Then there will be righteous sacrifices,
  whole burnt offerings to delight you;
  then bulls will be offered on your
    altar.

So eventually David had to accept that his first rather clumsy attempt at a cover-up wasn't going to work. And that's when he decided upon a much more brazen and disgraceful strategy of concealment: First, instruct commander-in-chief Joab to engineer events in such a way that Uriah was killed in battle. Second, after a suitable funeral, with full military honors, marry the poor grieving widow. Third, adopt her unborn child as a prince of the royal line, a fittingly gracious gesture to the memory of a national hero like Uriah.

If his first cover-up had been clumsy, this alternative ploy was unscrupulous, cynical, and sordid. Watergate and Irangate pale into Sunday school picnics by comparison. But it did work. Uriah died; Bathsheba was remarried to David; and the child was adopted. And there, I guess, David hoped it would all end. He may have broken at least three of the Ten Commandments, but he had managed to keep the eleventh—thou shalt not be found out! Of course, General Joab and some of his staff knew about it all, but they wouldn't be so stupid as to leak it to the press. There was no mole in David's staff. He had covered his tracks very professionally; Machiavelli would have been proud of him. It was an unfortunate episode, of course, but then there is no use crying over spilt milk. Politics is a dirty business. There are a few skeletons in most royal cupboards. It had happened, it was over, and now it could be forgotten.

But that, of course, was where David made his biggest mistake, bigger even than the crimes of adultery and deceit and murder that he had so callously committed. Sin can't be confined to the past in that easy way. Even if the courts don't penalize it, even if public scandals don't expose it, even if we manage to carry on the hypocrisy as David probably did, doing our job, going to church, saying our prayers, reading our Bibles, just as if it had never happened at all, still the skeleton is there, rotting away in the cupboard. And sooner or later the stink will seep out through the cracks and start to choke us. You can't cover up guilt no matter how hard you try. The only safe thing you can do with guilt is to have it washed away. And there is only one Person in the world with the spiritual detergent necessary to erase such stains.

David learned that lesson eventually. He learned it through a preacher called Nathan, who came to call on him one day and confronted him with his sin. Psalm 51, according to its heading in the

Hebrew Bible, is the poem David wrote in the wake of that humiliating exposure. He writes it for us, surely, so that we may share his experience.

If we are going to deal with guilt successfully, four things are necessary: First, we must face something; second, we must do something; third, we must want something; and fourth, we must believe something.

We Must Face Something

The thing we must face, of course, is the guilt itself: "I know my transgressions, and my sin is always before me" (v. 3). He had tried to cover it up before. That's what we all do. But the first thing he had to learn, before he could cope with this guilt properly and get it out of his system, was to look inside his heart and face up to the truth he found there. Of course that isn't always an easy experience. Self-examination is tough. It is rather like the story of an old mountaineer who had never seen much of civilization. One day while he was wandering on his mountain, he found a mirror. He had never seen a mirror before, so when he looked at his reflection, he said, "My word, if it isn't a picture of my old pappy!" He took the mirror home, thoroughly pleased with it, and hid it in his private possessions. About a week later, his wife was searching through his private possessions and found the mirror. She looked into it and said, "Huh, so that's the ugly old witch he's been going around with behind my back all these years!"

It can be a shock to see ourselves as we really are. We may think ourselves beautiful and look in a mirror only to find that we are actually ugly old witches. Oliver Cromwell, when he commissioned his portrait, told the artist to paint him just as he was, "warts and all." But most of us would rather be flattered.

I suppose there are a few psychopathic personalities that can actually take pride in their sins, like the man who was arrested in Mexico while admiring his picture on a wanted poster outside the police station. But most of us, when our consciences prick us like David's did, turn to the cosmetics cupboard and find something to cover it up. In fact, we have devised quite a lot of little aids in our subterfuge.

Excuses

There is the powder-puff of our excuses, for instance. Even Adam and Eve tried to pass the buck. Adam blamed Eve; Eve blamed the serpent; the serpent hadn't a leg to stand on! Perhaps it is because this particular technique of evasion goes back so far in our memory that it comes quickly to us. A child has hardly learned to talk before it has learned to make excuses. And of course, modern thought has increased our repertoire of excuses enormously. Freud has taught us that we can blame our parents; Marx has taught us that we can blame the capitalist system. We can blame our hormones; we can even blame our diet these days.

Did David rationalize his sin, I wonder? Did he blame Bathsheba for getting pregnant? "How could you be so careless? It's all your fault!" Did he blame Uriah for being so noble? "What an idiot that man is! Can't he see I'm trying to help him?" I expect he did. Excuses usually come very easily to our lips.

Righteous Indignation

If blaming others doesn't work, there is always the masking cream of righteous indignation. Like the Pharisees we read about in the New Testament who hid behind a hypocritical smokescreen of virtuosity and respectability, we can point out our moral record—all the good things we've done, all the bad things we haven't done. We can point out how much better we are than some people we might mention. We can wax eloquent about the decay in moral standards and the need for law and order. I expect David did a bit of that, too. I bet you he was hard on anybody who came up before him in the courts, charged with adultery or murder, that spring season. There is a story about a Sunday school teacher who was warning his children about the dangers of the Pharisees. He ended up by saying, "Now, children, let's thank God we are not like those self-righteous Pharisees!"

Repression

Perhaps the most dangerous form of cover-up is the eau-de-cologne of repression. It is modern psychiatry that has taught us that word. Instead of trying to argue our way out of guilt by excuses or downright denial, we erect subtler, psychological defenses against the truth. We bury our guilt in some subconscious corner of our minds. And of course, psychiatrists are right when they say that when that happens, guilt festers away and reappears in ways that are not obviously related to the original sin at all.

Most of us have met folks with inferiority complexes, the type of people who are always running themselves down, who don't feel that they are worth anything. Whatever you say to them, they interpret it as a put-down. Sometimes they have a masochistic streak and feel they need to punish themselves. Or sometimes they deliberately organize their lives in such a way that misfortune befalls them. "There," they say, "I deserved that."

Such people may be so pathetic in their feelings of unworthiness that you might think they are excessively guilt-ridden, rather than guilt avoiding. But actually, when you dig a little deeper, often what you find is that it is precisely to convey such an impression that they adopt a policy of self-recrimination. By condemning themselves in this habitual way, they extract sympathy and support from others and divert attention from the ugliness in their lives that they dare not admit even to themselves. It is easier to feel generalized remorse and self-pity all the time, than to face up to the real guilt that we bury deep down in our hearts.

Perfectionists represent another example of this kind of repressed guilt. These people have to be correct about everything, no matter how trifling the detail. Their house will be spotless; it has to be, since the tiniest mark on the carpet generates huge anxiety. They will be fastidious in their clothes. Sometimes they will even develop little rituals, obsessively washing their hands a hundred times a day, or constantly disinfecting the toilet. It is all really an elaborate conspiracy designed to create an illusion of impeccability, when the truth is that deep down they are burdened by a great weight of sin that they dare not expose to public gaze.

I suspect David suffered some of these neurotic consequences of repressed guilt; that's why he speaks in verse 8 of "the bones you have crushed." No matter how well he played his role in public, you can't tell me he didn't suffer the private emotional pain that repressed guilt always brings: the anxiety, the depression, the aches and pains, the ulcers, and the hypertension. Inwardly he was a wreck. What psychological penetration he displays when he says, "God desires truth in the inner parts . . . wisdom in the inmost place." If we are going to find peace of mind and heart, that's where the work has to be done. The truth has to come out; what's buried in those inmost places has to be exposed; the cosmetic cover-up, the rationalizations of our feeble excuses, the sanctimonious self-righteousness that we present as a smokescreen all have to be abandoned. Repression has to give way to confession; we have to face up to the reality of our guilt. And for many of us, that first step is the most difficult.

We Must Do Something

What we must do, of course, is to have personal dealings with God about our guilt. See what David says in verse 4: "Against you, you only, have I sinned and done what is evil in your sight, so that you are proved right when you speak and justified when you judge." Some people find fault with David in that line, "You only have I sinned against." What about Bathsheba, hadn't he sinned against her? What about Uriah? But David is expressing here the truth that every sinner ultimately has to accept. In the final analysis, our sin is against God, and God only. We cannot come to terms with our guilt until we have personal dealings with God about it.

Contrary to what many psychiatrists today will tell you, guilt is not just a psychological hang-up; it is something objective, something real, that stands between my Maker and me. The God who rules this universe is not some impersonal energy; he is a moral Being, a holy Judge. When we do things wrong, we offend God. We are not just transgressing human social conventions; it is not just the superego of our internalized parental dependencies that we are flouting. No, we are offending God.

Those prickings of conscience we feel are the reflection in us of divine moral sensitivity. So it is not enough that the psychotherapist can help us to come to terms with our guilt. It is not enough even that the human being that we have hurt by our sin forgives us. I am not my own judge and neither are they. I stand accountable before God's bar of justice. "You are proved right when you speak and justified when you judge," says David. "Against you, you only, have I sinned."

This is so important. Many people think that they are confessing their sins when all they are really experiencing is wounded pride. "I let myself down then," they say. "My estimate of myself has been deflated. I am angry with myself. I should have done better." They think they are confessing their sins when all they are really feeling is remorse at the consequences that their mistakes have plunged them into. "Oh, I should have known I'd never get away with it," they say.

But it isn't enough to be angry with yourself, for whatever reason. We have to face up to the fact that God is angry. It is not enough to be sorry for ourselves; we have to face the fact that it is God we have injured. We can only really begin to come to terms with guilt when our minds are no longer absorbed by thoughts of how our sin affects us, or even how our sin affects other people, and we start to take seriously and feel burdened about how our sin is affecting God.

We Must Want Something

Here, perhaps, is the most common sticking point of all. The third step is that we must want to change. Look at verses 7–10:

> Cleanse me with hyssop, and I will be clean;
>   wash me, and I will be whiter than snow.
> Let me hear joy and gladness;
>   let the bones you have crushed rejoice.
> Hide your face from my sins
>   and blot out all my iniquity.
>
> Create in me a pure heart, O God,
>   and renew a steadfast spirit within me.

There is a danger in what we have said already about feeling our guilt and facing up to it: The danger is that we shall wallow in it. There can be a certain self-indulgence in negative feelings about ourselves. As long as we keep looking inside ourselves and bemoaning how miserable we are, it is very easy to become increasingly absorbed in self-pity. But that won't do. If there's going to be a way out of our guilt, we have to want things to be different. That means we have to want to change.

David expresses this by using the word *hyssop* (v. 7). In the Old Testament, the priests used hyssop to purify a leper. If a man was cleansed of his leprosy, there was a prescribed ceremony whereby he could be declared clean and sent back into the community. What David is saying here is that he feels the defilement of his sin like leprosy. Perhaps these days AIDS would be the equivalent of leprosy. A vicious and ugly infection in his personality is taking him to a shameful death. He longs for healing; he longs for cleansing; he longs to be rehabilitated, just like a cleansed leper, and sent back into the community.

This is surely more than poetic imagery. As we've already seen, David knew that a human being is a psychosomatic whole; there is no sharp dividing line between the health of the body and the health of the soul. Guilt destroys our wholeness. Often it does produce real, physical symptoms. We can only be psychologically, physically, and spiritually whole when the garbage-heap of these repressed and rationalized and hidden sins of ours are cleaned up and washed away.

David is under no illusions about just how radical the necessary therapy must be. See how he describes it in verse 10: "Create in me a pure heart." Here's a heart transplant that exceeds anything you'll find in modern cardiac surgery. David is asking for a miracle. He uses the word *create* knowing only God can create. *Heart* and *spirit* are the words Hebrews used for the center of the human will and mind. And it is there that David says he needs to see not just superficial Elastoplast, but total renewal. "Create in me a pure heart." As he has meditated on his sin, David has come to realize just how deep the infection is embedded in him. It goes far beyond those specific acts associated with this dreadful affair of Bathsheba and Uriah. In verse 5 he recognizes, "I was sinful at birth, sinful at the time my mother conceived me."

Guilt is not something that adheres like some fungus on the surface of our lives that we can scrape off. It is not something that we can separate ourselves from. It is a defect of our very personality and character. It is the corruption of our very nature. It is something we are quite literally born with. "A fundamental selfishness and rebelliousness," says David, "which has been evident from the very moment I emerged from the womb." There are simply no resources in us to combat this depth of depravity; there is no little island of innocence in our personalities from which we can launch our counter-offensive, no tiny reservoir of moral power by which to exorcise the demon in us. Our wills are corrupt, our emotions are corrupt, our minds are corrupt. The very core of the human personality is twisted by sin. Even when there was only one cell of me adhering to the wall of my mother's uterus, sin was there, in some mysterious way, pro-grammed into that embryonic existence. That is the extent of our plight as human beings. It is more than a minor repair job we need; it is a complete moral overhaul. It is not just isolated acts of sin that we need to be cleansed from; it is the powerful grip of sin on our whole lives.

Our problem, so often, is that we don't want to pray, "Create in me a pure heart," because we don't want to change in that radical way. Maybe we would like God's help over some particularly deep prob-lem that we have gotten ourselves into. But God won't do that with-out going on to demand far more. If you give him an inch, he takes a mile. He is in the business of creating pure hearts, not just patching up little bits of our lives.

That's why we shrink back. That's why we prefer our cover-ups. We want to stay as we are. At the back of our minds there is the thought, "I would really like to sin again." Like dirty children rolling in the mud we don't *want* to be clean, we don't *want* a pure heart. Perhaps that's why David prays, "Grant me a willing spirit" in verse 12. Maybe that's the prayer we need to pray. Even the desire to be clean is something, if the truth be known, that God has to put inside us. And until he has put it there, we're helpless, for we don't even want to be different.

We Must Believe Something

Here is the fourth and final step. We have to believe that God will accept us.

> You do not delight in sacrifice, or I would bring it;
>   you do not take pleasure in burnt offerings.
> The sacrifices of God are a broken spirit;
>   a broken and contrite heart,
>   O God, you will not despise (51:16–17).

41

Why not? Why shouldn't God despise a broken and a contrite heart? Flowing through this psalm is an extraordinary confidence in God's willingness to forgive. Even in verse 7 where in our translation the verbs are expressed as imperatives—cleanse me, wash me—you could equally correctly render them as future tenses—you will cleanse me, you will wash me. This psalm is an affirmation of faith, just as much as it is a plea for mercy. And it is that assurance that David articulates again when he insists, "A broken and contrite heart, O God, you will not despise."

How could David be so sure about that? Perhaps the clue is in verse 12: "Restore to me the joy of your salvation." That word *restore* reminds us that God was no stranger to David. David could recall times when things had been different between them, when they had enjoyed an intimate and personal communion with one another. And more than anything else in the world, David longs for the restoration of that relationship. That's why he says in verse 11, "Do not cast me from your presence or take your Holy Spirit from me." Or, "Whatever you do, God, don't abandon me."

I suspect that a horrible memory haunted David as he meditated about his sin—the memory of King Saul, his predecessor in office. Saul had been anointed by God; Saul had been filled with the Spirit of God just like David. But David knew that Saul had ended his life demented, vicious, pathetic; for Saul had proudly defied God, and God had deserted Saul. David was terrified by that memory; so should we be. There is no room for complacency in this psalm; guilt is dangerous, and David knows it. Guilt can drive the Holy Spirit from us; guilt can alienate us from God's presence. Guilt can shut and bar the doors of heaven to us. Guilt can rob us of the greatest bliss any human being can know: the bliss of knowing God personally. David had known that bliss and was desperate at the thought of losing it. But he knew that his sin was so heinous that he could lose it. God in perfect justice could abandon him just as he had abandoned Saul.

Yet in spite of that, welling up from somewhere in David, triumphing over his despair, there is a confidence that it will not be so. This psalm is a prayer of faith, not a suicide note. "All I've got is a broken and a contrite heart," he says, "but I'm absolutely sure God won't despise that." David had learned something about God's character that Saul never seems to have learned. It is there right at the beginning of the psalm; it is the very basis on which he begins his plea: "Have mercy on me, O God, according to your unfailing love; according to your great compassion blot out my transgressions."

Love and *compassion*—these are words of tenderness. These are the feelings of a father for his child. David knew such feelings lay in the heart of God toward him. That's why he could say so confidently, "A broken and contrite heart, O God, you will not despise." Even though in justice, God could have banished him from his presence and sent him to hell, yet in the very depths of his being, David found this faith welling up: God will accept me. There is unfailing love and compassion in the heart of God, even for me.

And you and I have to believe that too. If we don't, we will despair as Saul despaired. This is the difference between a believer and an unbeliever. Unbelievers feel guilty too, but they don't know what to do with their guilt, for they cannot, like David, experience justification by faith.

Where does such faith come from? Maybe you are saying to yourself, "Yes, I feel guilty; I know I've got to have dealings with God about it. I'd like to change, I really would. But how can I be sure that God will accept me? How can I be sure that if I dare to come to God and confess these terrible things that I know are lurking inside me, that he's not going to slap me in the face and tell me to get lost?" All David had to go on was a few books of the Old Testament and his personal experience, beginning as a shepherd boy. You and I have something better. We have the blood of Jesus. God put him on the cross so that in his agony we might see that there is unfailing love and compassion in the heart of God for sinners. The blood he shed is God's pledge that he can and will forgive the penitent. *Do you believe it?* That's the crunch issue! We have to believe that forgiveness is available, even though we simultaneously have to accept that we have no right to claim it. Forgiveness is something that God gives to us as a free gift. We seek it, like David, on our knees. We can't claim it like unemployment benefits. And yet forgiveness is dependable for all that. It's not automatic, for we must ask for it. Yet we may have confidence that we will receive it—not because we deserve it, but because of the kind of God he is—a God of unfailing love and compassion.

When Nathan came to David and confronted him with his sin, David's heart was on trial. He could have told Nathan to get lost; he could have become angry; he could have executed Nathan on the spot for insolence, just as King Herod did to John the Baptist. David's heart was on trial as he responded to that prophetic message. So our hearts are on trial too. What are we going to do about our guilt? Bury it? Cover it up? Continue this insane hypocrisy as if nothing is wrong? David shows us a better way: face up to it, have dealings with God about it, desire change, and believe that he will accept you. You will find, like David, that you'll be able to say, "Then I will teach transgressors your ways, and sinners will turn back to you. . . . Lord, open my lips, and my mouth will declare your praise."

3

PRAYING THROUGH YOUR ANXIETY

How do you cope in a crisis? Kipling, of course, praised the manly virtue of the person who could keep his head when all about were losing theirs. Privately, I suspect, we all share his admiration for that kind of unruffled composure even if, unlike him, we don't think it's the prerogative of the male sex. If only we could sail through the storms of life, calm and serene. If only we could be one of those people who are able to sleep at night no matter what slings and arrows outrageous fortune may hurl into their paths. That is all a big *If,* as Kipling himself implied by the title of that famous poem.

Most of us aren't like that. That is why managing directors command such high salaries. People who can cope with high levels of stress are a rarity. There is a shortage in the market for such people. Indeed, if the truth be known, many who aspire to executive posts achieve their image of unflappable poise only by virtue of the tranquilizers they cram into the top drawer of their desks. Anxiety comes naturally to human beings. We each have different tolerances; some of us are more vulnerable to pressure than others. But everybody's mental and emotional constitution has its limitations. You only have to study the incidence of combat fatigue in time of war to realize that. Nobody, no matter how courageous in spirit, is immune to the so-called nervous breakdown. If any of us are placed in a situation of sufficient stress, we will crack. And that goes for the Christian just as much as for the non-Christian.

There are some superspiritual types who want to deny that. Didn't Jesus rebuke his disciples for their worried frowns, didn't he chasten them by the example of the birds of the air and the lilies of the field for their pointless fretting? Of course he did. But if you think about it, the mere fact that he asks in that famous passage, "Why do you worry?" is clear evidence that he knew we would *suffer* from anxiety. It may be incongruous for a Christian to worry; it may expose, as Jesus said, the shallowness of our faith, or the worldliness of our aspirations. But there is nothing about being a Christian that immunizes a person against the experience of anxiety. If there were, Jesus would never have had to bother talking about it. The truth is that Christians do battle with worry just as everybody else does. You only have to look into the experience of great saints, both in the Bible and outside it, to realize that.

Psalm 55

[1]Listen to my prayer, O God,
    do not ignore my plea;
[2] hear me and answer me.
My thoughts trouble me and I am
    distraught
[3] at the voice of the enemy,
    at the stares of the wicked;
for they bring down suffering upon me
    and revile me in their anger.

[4]My heart is in anguish within me;
    the terrors of death assail me.

[5]Fear and trembling have beset me;
    horror has overwhelmed me.
[6]I said, "Oh, that I had the wings of a
    dove!
    I would fly away and be at rest—
[7]I would flee far away
    and stay in the desert;   *Selah*
[8]I would hurry to my place of shelter,
    far from the tempest and storm."

[9]Confuse the wicked, O Lord, confound
    their speech,
for I see violence and strife in the city.

46

[10]Day and night they prowl about on its
    walls;
  malice and abuse are within it.
[11]Destructive forces are at work in the
    city;
  threats and lies never leave its streets.

[12]If an enemy were insulting me,
  I could endure it;
if a foe were raising himself against me,
  I could hide from him.
[13]But it is you, a man like myself,
  my companion, my close friend,
[14]with whom I once enjoyed sweet
    fellowship
  as we walked with the throng at the
    house of God.

[15]Let death take my enemies by surprise;
  let them go down alive to the grave,
  for evil finds lodging among them.

[16]But I call to God,
  and the LORD saves me.
[17]Evening, morning and noon
  I cry out in distress,
  and he hears my voice.

[18]He ransoms me unharmed
  from the battle waged against me,
  even though many oppose me.
[19]God, who is enthroned forever,
  will hear them and afflict them—
                                    Selah
men who never change their ways
  and have no fear of God.

[20]My companion attacks his friends;
  he violates his covenant.
[21]His speech is smooth as butter,
  yet war is in his heart;
his words are more soothing than oil,
  yet they are drawn swords.

[22]Cast your cares on the LORD
  and he will sustain you;
  he will never let the righteous fall.
[23]But you, O God, will bring down the
    wicked
  into the pit of corruption;
bloodthirsty and deceitful men
  will not live out half their days.

But as for me, I trust in you.

The difference faith makes is not that it makes us impervious to stress, but that it gives us an additional resource in time of stress, a resource that the unbeliever doesn't have. It is a resource that in troubled circumstances can make the difference, to use Kipling's words, between keeping your head and losing it.

In Psalm 55 we have a perfect example of that resource being employed in just one such crisis situation. It is clear from several of the things that David says in this psalm that it was composed at a period of great personal insecurity in his life. He speaks repeatedly of enemies who are wickedly plotting his downfall. He speaks in particular of the treachery of one whom he had formerly regarded as a friend, but who now was apparently the ringleader of this callous conspiracy. It is difficult to be sure what particular incident in David's long and varied life might be in view. We know from the books of 1 and 2 Samuel that for many years he was on the run from the jealous hatred of King Saul, and undoubtedly there were critical moments of betrayal and danger during that time that might have provided the background for a psalm like this. But the mention of the word *city* in verse 9 and again in verse 11 would argue against identifying the psalm with that early period of David's life. If the city in question is Jerusalem, then it must come from the period after he had come to the throne of Israel when Jerusalem had become his capital. And if so, then the most likely context of this psalm is during one of those many attempted coups that David suffered in the latter years of his reign. Perhaps the most likely candidate is the one when his own son, Absalom, conspired against him.

Whatever the precise situation was, David was in big trouble, and like anybody else in such a situation of stress, he worried about it. Indeed, worry is perhaps too moderate a term. It would be closer to the mark to say he was in a state of total panic: "My heart is in anguish within me; the terrors of death assail me. Fear and trembling have beset me; horror has overwhelmed me" (vv. 4–5). Maybe it is reassuring to some of us to know the extremity of emotional devastation that David felt. After all the man who slew Goliath was no coward. The man who wrote "The Lord is my shepherd" had a close walk with God. If a man as brave and as spiritual as David could be victim to such an overwhelming attack of anxiety, then clearly Christians need not feel guilty when they pass through similar experiences. Faith didn't immunize David against worry. Anxiety was still there in his repertoire of emotional responses just as it is in everybody's.

The Resource of Prayer

> Listen to my prayer, O God,
>   do not ignore my plea;
>   hear me and answer me (55:1).

Prayer is the distinctive resource that the believer has that the unbeliever cannot share.

I am not suggesting, of course, that if you are worrying about something, all you need to do is to recite a few sentences with the word *Amen* on the end, and all those anxieties will automatically dissolve away. It wasn't like that for David, and it won't be like that for you and me. When I say that prayer is a resource in these times of trouble and emotional crisis, what I mean is that prayer provides a context in which we can work through our anxieties and come to terms with them. Indeed, that is just what we see David doing in this psalm, in a particularly transparent manner.

When you read the psalm you will see that there are a number of diverse elements in it that seem to be thrown together in a rather haphazard way. There are sections that speak of intense fear and danger, like verses 4 and 5. There are sections that speak of David's hostility toward his enemies who were threatening him, as in verses 9–11 or again in verses 12–15. There are sections that speak of David's grief at his friend's betrayal, like verses 12–14 and again in verses 20–21. And mixed in with all these negative feelings, there are sections that confess great confidence in God. The interesting thing is that these elements are muddled up. David seems to swing wildly between them. Sometimes he almost breaks off in mid-sentence and launches on a different tack so that the reader is left suspended in mid-air. There is no logical, clear development through this psalm. Panic and sorrow, anger and faith do battle in the text. The poet seems to rebound from one emotion to another, a bit like a football in a school playground.

Predictably, there are a number of Old Testament scholars who observe this disjointedness and conclude that the text is dislocated. The psalm has been cut up, added to, pulled around, and generally massacred by so many authors and editors that it looks more like a pastiche of fragments, stuck with glue in a scrapbook, than a single, coherent, and carefully constructed poem. Quite frankly, scholars like that just need to get their noses out of their Hebrew lexicons and into a bit of pastoral counseling! For if they did that, they would quickly realize that the erratic oscillations that characterize this psalm represent precisely the sort of collision of contradictory emotions that marks anybody passing through a situation of extreme stress.

Of course the psalm lacks logical coherence, but at this particular point in his life David lacked logical coherence! He was a seething mass of inner confusion. He tells us himself: "My thoughts trouble me and I am distraught" (v. 2). This psalm wasn't written by David in the calm tranquillity of hindsight; this psalm was written with the thunder and lightning of his agonized emotions bursting around his head. This isn't a man reflecting on the experience of anxiety after the trouble is all over; this is a man actually wrestling with the experience of anxiety in the midst of trouble. That is what makes the psalm so peculiarly interesting. It isn't just telling us that prayer *can* make a difference when we are experiencing trouble. It shows us how prayer *did* make a difference to a man who was in trouble. It is a model to us of prayer at work in a crisis experience. These ill-shaped elements that alternate so wildly are not evidence of textual dislocation at all. They are clues to a proper understanding of the psalm and a proper emotional engagement with David in his writing of it. Here is a man struggling with a torrent of feelings that deluge him one after another. But he is not struggling with them as an unbeliever must in the isolation of his own private hell. Instead, David is struggling with these feelings as only a believer can, in the intimate, one-to-one relationship of his prayer life with God. The reason this psalm is included in the Psalter is because he wants to commend such a policy to us so that we may share his discovery. Verse 22 is the key: "Cast your cares on the LORD and he will sustain you," just as he sustained David.

Let's pick out just two of those diverse elements we have noted that fly around inside this psalm: fear and hostility. Let's see just how David prayed through each of them.

Feelings of Fear

> My thoughts trouble me and I am distraught
>> at the voice of the enemy,
>> at the stares of the wicked;
> for they bring down suffering upon me
>> and revile me in their anger.
>
> My heart is in anguish within me;
>> the terrors of death assail me.

> Fear and trembling have beset me;
>   horror has overwhelmed me (55:2b–5).

Quite clearly this was not a mild attack of nerves. This is what a twentieth century psychiatrist would label as an acute anxiety attack. All the symptoms are there. For a start there is mental confusion. The Hebrew of verse 2 conveys the idea of thoughts madly rushing about, a kind of distracted restlessness. Anxiety always generates such bewilderment. "I can't concentrate," we say. "I'm in a spin, my mind is racing." Habitual suspiciousness is another common characteristic: ". . . the voice of the enemy, the stares of the wicked; for they bring down suffering upon me and revile me in their anger" (v. 3). David's awareness of the palace plot was breeding paranoia in him. He felt as though he were surrounded by a sea of secret antagonism and ill will. Wherever he went, he sensed people's eyes upon him. He heard them whispering their conspiracy against him behind his back.

Then there is the emotional torture that he describes in verses 4 and 5. David piles word upon word here, to try to express the intensity of his inner pain: "My heart is in anguish," "terrors of death," "fear and trembling," "horror." Literally what he says in verse 4 in the Hebrew is "My heart writhes in my guts." It is as if all his inner organs have twisted themselves into knots. The awful foreboding of imminent death hangs over him like a sword of Damocles: "I feel as if at any moment I am going to be struck down dead, and as a result I am jumpy, I am irritable, I can't sleep, I am breaking out in cold sweats, my heartbeat is irregular, my stomach is brewing ulcers, my blood pressure is sky-high, my head aches." This is what anxiety feels like, and David knows it. Only those who have gone through such a dreadful experience can know how tormenting it is. Several people I have talked to who have had this sort of acute anxiety attack have told me they would, quite seriously, rather die than have a recurrence.

The Desire to Escape

It is no wonder that all David can think of is escape.

> I said, "Oh, that I had the wings of a dove!
>   I would fly away and be at rest—

> I would flee far away
>   and stay in the desert;   *Selah*
> I would hurry to my place of shelter,
>   far from the tempest and storm" (55:6–8).

This is really so characteristic of an anxiety state that I am quite sure that any who have passed through such an experience will be quietly nodding to themselves as they read it. "I must get away," says David. "I can't take this constant pressure of worry and anxiety anymore. I must find relief or I shall go mad." Yet, paradoxically, it is that imperative desire for escape that represents one of the most dangerous dimensions of anxiety.

Up to a point, escape is a necessary and normal response to worry. We all escape in a sense without realizing it every night when we go to sleep and dream. Dreams constitute a kind of safety valve; they purge the emotional pressure from our lives. In more conscious ways, too, we escape when we take our annual vacation, when we play sports, when we read a book, or when we watch a film. But it is characteristic of all those safe modes of escape that the situation generating the anxiety is only temporarily abandoned. We waken out of our dream, we return from our vacation, we emerge from the football stadium or the cinema, and we face real life again. We haven't run away from the problem totally, just taken a therapeutic break from it.

That's good, but when anxiety is really acute, there is a temptation to flee our problem permanently. We may, for instance, try to perpetuate a dream state in our waking moments, through alcohol or narcotics. In some cases, people try to perpetuate the holiday mood by dropping out of society, or by falling into a "fugue" state of spontaneous amnesia. Most commonly we simply try to deny our anxious feelings altogether, to block the whole painful business from our thoughts, to switch off that bit of circuitry in our brains. This is what psychiatrists mean when they talk about repressing anxiety into the subconscious.

Such strategies of total escape are very tempting, but they are always self-defeating because, of course, we can't run away from our feelings. Our feelings are part of us. When we try to build a barricade between ourselves and our feelings, all we are really doing is creating a kind of inner alienation within ourselves; and that generates more problems than it solves. What happens, for instance, when we repress anxiety and won't face up to it, is that it corrodes our peace of mind like a kind of psychological acid. Some people get depressed, some people become hypochondriac, some people develop irrational phobias or psychosomatic illnesses, and so on. Though we may want to flee our anxious feelings, escape is no real answer. And to give David credit, in this particular crisis, he recognized as much: "A dove maybe could find refuge in this situation, but a human being can't," he says. "If I were a dove, I would fly away. Yet it is all hypothetical, for the fact is, I am stuck here with no way out. Much as I might want to escape, I can't."

God's Listening Ear

This is the first reason prayer was so important for David. It provided a forum in which he could verbalize his frustration about being trapped in the situation. Prayer saved David from the need to repress his anxiety and provided him with a way of expressing it. There is a great deal of truth in the old maxim that a trouble shared is a trouble halved. Often the thing we will do on a human level, when we have anxieties, is to find somebody we can talk to about it because that eases the problem. But sometimes, of course, there isn't anybody around with whom we can share our trouble; we feel isolated in our distress just as David did. We feel that there is nobody we can trust. That is when the believer has an extra resource; he is never totally alone; he is never without a sympathetic ear into which he can pour the sorry tale of his anguish. He has God's ear: "Listen to my prayer, O God, do not ignore my plea; hear me and answer me." Prayer gives us access to the best listener in the world.

David says in verse 17: "Evening, morning and noon I cry out in distress, and he hears my voice." Derek Kidner suggests in his little commentary that the reference to morning, noon, and night may be more than just a poetic idiom. He feels it may reflect a literal discipline of prayer that David imposed upon himself during this crisis period, like Daniel who opened his window and got down on his knees three times a day to pray. Maybe that is right. Certainly, there can be no question that David found in regular and frequent times of prayer a means by which he could work through the anxiety that was threatening to destroy him.

The same can be true for us. This is what Paul wrote in Philippians 4:6–7:

> Do not be anxious about anything, but in everything, by prayer and petition, with thanksgiving, present your requests to God. And the peace of God, which transcends all understanding, will guard your hearts and your minds in Christ Jesus.

He is not saying that we should feel guilty as Christians because we are anxious. What he is saying is that when Christians are anxious, they have a resource they can turn to that the unbeliever doesn't have—prayer. Make use of it! It is not that the Christian is incapable of anxiety, but that he knows what to do about his feelings of anxiety. He has somewhere he can work through them. He doesn't have to repress them; he doesn't have to escape them. He can talk about them to God, and that is exactly what we see David doing here. I expect as David walked around his palace you would never have guessed the inner anguish that was going on inside him. I bet you would have thought, "Wow! What a calm, composed fellow he is!" But if you saw David on his own, on his knees, you would discover the secret of that composure: "Cast your cares on the Lord and he will sustain you."

Feelings of Hostility

> Confuse the wicked, O Lord, confound their speech,
>   for I see violence and strife in the city.
> Day and night they prowl about on its walls;
>   malice and abuse are within it.
> Destructive forces are at work in the city;
>   threats and lies never leave its streets.
>
> Let death take my enemies by surprise;
>   let them go down alive to the grave,
>   for evil finds lodging among them (55:9–11, 15).

There are many examples of verses like this in the psalms: imprecatory cries for vengeance. Many people profess to find it a problem that such sentiments should be expressed in the Bible. Surely, they say, this kind of vindictiveness is out of keeping with what the Bible has to say about loving one another and forgiving our enemies. There are several things arising from this psalm that can be said in response to that.

God's Enemies

The first thing to note is that David is calling down judgment on these individuals, not because they are his enemies, primarily, but because they are God's enemies. Notice, for instance in verses 10–11, the concern for social justice that is informing his indignation. "There is violence and strife in the city," he says. "It's not just against me; it is infecting society. Day and night violence and strife are prowling about on its walls; malice and abuse are within it; destructive forces are at work in the city; threats and lies never leave its streets." It is quite clear that this conspiracy against David was having a demoralizing effect on the whole community. Acts of terrorism, intimidation, and corruption were undermining the fabric of law and order. It is often that way: revolution and anarchy are blood brothers. David sees their affiliation working out in his beloved city of Jerusalem, and that outrages him.

It should outrage us, too. The idea that anger is necessarily a sinful emotion is quite mistaken; on the contrary, there are things it would be sinful *not* to be angry about. We ought to be angry at cruelty, at injustice, at exploitation. It is no virtue to be complacent, apathetic, or indifferent in the face of such things. You have only to remember how Jesus drove the money changers out of the temple to be clear about that. Righteousness was the fundamental issue in David's mind too, not personal pique or insecurity.

God's Judgment

The second thing to note is that David is really only asking God to act here in a way that is consistent with his judgment against sin down through history. In fact, in this psalm David makes two oblique allusions to actual incidents in the Old Testament.

First, in verse 9 he says: "Confuse the wicked, O Lord, confound their speech." That may very well be a reference to the Tower of Babel and the judgment that God brought upon it. There God frustrated the dangerous ambition of godless men by erecting communication barriers between them and setting them at cross-purposes to one another.

"You did that once, God," David is saying. "Well, do it again, because I can see the same kind of reckless evil at work in my society as threatened Babel."

Second, in verse 15 he says: "Let death take my enemies by surprise; let them go down alive to the grave." That too is almost certainly a reference to the judgment of Korah in the Book of Numbers. Korah rebelled against Moses and was swallowed by some kind of fissure in the earth as punishment. David is again saying, "You did it once, God. Do it again, because exactly the same kind of rebellion against the authorities that you have appointed is going on now."

Down through history God has been active repeatedly in judgment against unrighteousness in humans. Again and again, what David says in verse 23 has proved to be true: "You, O God, will bring down the wicked . . . bloodthirsty and deceitful men will not live out half their days." David is asking no more than that God should vindicate himself against wickedness in the same kind of way he had always done. We must not confuse love for our enemies with sentimentality about moral evil and the reality of divine judgment. God does judge. It was Jesus himself who said, echoing David, that those who live by the sword, die by the sword. Such is the nature of the moral universe God has made.

More Than Feelings

The third thing about these imprecatory comments we find here is that the anger and hostility that David felt, even insofar as it did focus around his own sense of injury, was not just an irrational feeling. It is not as if David was flying off the handle without good cause. It is quite clear that he had been treated abominably. That comes out most clearly in those verses that speak of his grief at the involvement of his friend in this conspiracy.

> If an enemy were insulting me,
>   I could endure it;
> if a foe were raising himself against me,
>   I could hide from him.
> But it is you, a man like myself,
>   my companion, my close friend,
> with whom I once enjoyed sweet fellowship
>   as we walked with the throng at the house of God (55:12–14).

There is pathos in these words. Someone very close indeed to David was involved, and if our earlier speculation was right about the identity of this traitor, it adds even more poignancy to the situation.

What if when David speaks in verse 13 of a "man like myself" he were referring to none other than Prince Absalom, his own son? He was clearly somebody David was fond of—a colleague in his royal administration or a comrade with whom he had shared much of his life, at the very least. Indeed, it was a person he thought was a believer like him. They had gone to worship together so often, yet now this closest of friends had let him down. The promise of fidelity that they had made to one another was shattered. Though he was maintaining an appearance of courtesy and benevolence toward David, David knew it wasn't sincere any longer.

> My companion attacks his friends;
>   he violates his covenant.
> His speech is smooth as butter,
>   yet war is in his heart;
> his words are more soothing than oil,
>   yet they are drawn swords (55:20–21).

It doesn't take much to imagine how painful this was for David. Maybe some of us have been betrayed by people we were fond of in that same way. Our parents perhaps—we felt rejected by them. A husband or wife perhaps—they have been untrue to us. Few things inflict such a blow to our self-esteem as to be badly treated by those we thought loved us. When that rejection and infidelity is cloaked in deliberate deception and callous cruelty as it was here, the emotional injury is almost unbearable.

At least Julius Caesar hadn't the least knowledge of Brutus's part in the plot against his life until the moment of his assassination. Poor old David here was having to live with this facade of friendliness, day in and day out, knowing it all to be a sham. He could only wait for the moment when this so-called pal of his would make his move and try to stab him in the back. "I can handle naked enmity and aggression," says David. "I am a soldier, I understand war. But when the warfare concerned is hidden in the heart behind a veil of smooth talk and gushing amiability, it chokes me up."

In circumstances like that, hostility and anger are just reactions. Even if we may wish to argue that they fall below the example of Jesus, we can't blame David for feeling hostile when he had been abused in this way.

Private Prayer

The fourth, and perhaps the most important thing about these difficult, vengeful paragraphs, is that these hostile sentiments occur in the context of David's private prayers, not in the context of his public actions. That is really very significant. We don't have to read much of David's life history to appreciate how far from vindictiveness he really was. There have been few men, of his day or since, who have shown such generosity to their foes. Recall, for instance, the times he spared the life of his enemy Saul. David repeatedly refused to accept the opportunities fate gave him to dispose of this murderous maniac. Again and again David showed mercy when one would have thought political advantage was to be gained by surrendering to revenge (e.g., 1 Sam. 24:1–7; 26:5–12).

Or consider how he reacted over the incident of Absalom. When the news arrived that the rebellion had been crushed, and that Absalom had been killed, there was no "serves him right!" attitude. David, we are told, was visibly shaken. He went up to his private room, crying as he did so, "O my son Absalom! My son, my son Absalom! If only I had died instead of you—O Absalom, my son, my son!" (see 2 Sam. 18:31–19:8). David was not a spiteful man. In public actions, he was extraordinarily long-suffering.

How then are we to square the way he actually treated his enemies with these imprecatory sentiments in his psalms? Some will say that they are simply inconsistent. But a better response is to see these psalms as the psychological explanation of David's generosity of spirit. David wasn't an inhibited wimp who was incapable of feeling angry and hostile toward those who abused him. He felt furious just as any of us would. But instead of working out that rage through concrete acts of public spite, David worked those feelings through in intense moments of private prayer.

Dealing with Anger

This is so important. Psychiatrists have come to realize that anger is an immensely destructive emotion, and lies behind a great deal of the depression and anxiety that people suffer. Richard Winter, in his very useful book, *The Roots of Sorrow*, points out that until recently most psychiatrists were of the view that the only thing you could do with anger was to ventilate it: break a few plates, shout and scream, pummel a cushion, anything to get it off your chest. In fact many psychotherapies that are practiced today are designed to help people "get in touch with their feelings" in exactly this kind of way.

There is no doubt that some kind of emotional catharsis is often necessary when feelings of hostility have been bottled up for a long while. But more recent research has shown that, far from diffusing anger, these kinds of ventilating techniques often simply inflame anger. For instance, children who are encouraged to get rid of pent-up anger by kicking the furniture become more aggressive, not less, as time goes by. Couples who yell at one another don't feel less angry at the end of the week; they often feel more angry. For ventilation all too often simply fosters a settled habit of hostility, and instead of purging the grudge, it reinforces it.

What is needed is some way for a person to express anger without fueling it in the process. And that is precisely what David found in his prayer times. Some may feel that Jesus would never have prayed like this. Jesus would never have said, "Let death take my enemies by surprise; let them go down alive to the grave." And they're right, Jesus wouldn't. But David wasn't Jesus, and neither are we. Angry feelings are part of us. You may argue that they should not be part of us, and in an ideal world, perhaps they would not be. But the fact is they are there, and we have to do something with them. Bottling them up or denying that they exist is not the answer.

What David did was to express privately, in his prayers, exactly how he felt. That's what these imprecatory paragraphs are. "Sometimes I want to see my enemies dead," says David. If he had been a better man, maybe he wouldn't have felt like that. But the truth was he did feel like that, just as we all do sometimes. And nothing is to be gained by the pious pretense that we don't. Just as with his experience of fear and panic, prayer was providing David with a context in which he could express rather than repress those negative feelings that were being aroused by his situation of crisis and trouble.

Notice how in verse 13 he imaginatively enters into a dialogue with his treacherous friend, though clearly his friend is absent. "It is you," he says, "a man like myself." He is picturing his friend in front of his eyes as he is praying. For a moment the fact that David is praying to God seems to be almost forgotten. David is saying to his friend, through prayer, what in real life he couldn't say to him. Sometimes that is what prayer can be for us, and ought to be for us. There are times when we need to say things to people that we can't say; things that would be better left unsaid, but which from our point of view, need to be spoken. The unbeliever has nowhere to say them, except perhaps to his psychotherapist. David found, in prayer, the place he could do it. This is what David is inviting us to do when he says, "Cast your cares on the Lord."

If you are actually passing through a period of emotional crisis right now, I want to suggest that this psalm is of immense relevance. The feelings of panic and hostility that David is talking about are far from rare. Lots and lots of people suffer from them. He wants us to know the same experience that he found in wrestling with those feelings. "Cast your cares on the Lord," he says, "and he will sustain you." The problem with many of us is that we haven't learned how to do that. A friend of mine in Nairobi was driving a truck out in the bush one day when he met an old Kikuyu woman carrying a huge bundle of firewood on her head. It was clearly very heavy and she was tired, so my friend stopped the truck and asked her if she would like a lift. He was highly amused when he looked in the mirror after she had gotten on board. Though she was sitting in the back of the truck, the bundle of wood was still on her head! That is a picture, very often, of us. For some reason we don't want to cast our burden away. We nurse our negative feelings; we keep them until they become a great untameable monster in our imagination. David is showing us here how to use our prayer relationship with God in a situation of crisis to ground that emotional electricity, safely and harmlessly.

Some Christian counselors recommend that people going through emotional crises write a letter to God. Express to him the feelings that

60

are bottled up inside of you, the feelings that perhaps you don't really want to look in the face. Perhaps you can't possibly talk about the hostility you feel because the person to whom it is directed is a member of your family or a close friend. Write it down in a private letter to God. The guilt you feel, deriving from failures in the past or maybe in the present, makes you feel so dirty. You couldn't possibly admit it to anybody else. Write it down. Those memories that you dare not recall to mind because the moment your mind starts moving toward them, the pain is too great to bear. Force yourself to write it down. When you have finished your letter to God, offer it to him. Ask him to take it and deal with it. "Cast your cares on the Lord and he will hold you up."

Possibly there are some reading this chapter whose reaction will be one of quiet cynicism: "It is just as I thought; these Christians are a load of emotional inadequates. They can't get through life without a psychological crutch. They are so burdened by their anxiety feelings that they can't cope with them. They have to have a father-figure to lean on to get them through." I have met people who feel it is an evidence of weakness to pray because it stops people from relying on themselves and being strong.

If that is how you feel, I want you to come with me to a garden. There is a man in the garden, and just like David he is broken by inner conflict and by seething emotions. Just like David, he is being betrayed by one of his closest friends. Just like David, he has looked around the city of Jerusalem and has wept, for he has felt the weight of human sin and wickedness in that place. What is he doing? He is praying. Is he a cowardly wimp then? Is that your verdict? A man who needs the crutch of God to get him through this hour of crisis? Is he to be scorned for the immaturity of his infantile dependencies because at that moment in his life we find him saying "Father"?

I tell you this is the strongest man, the most *human* being that has ever walked the face of this globe. Of all men, this is the man we should most like to emulate. If he needed to pray, if he said to his disciples, "Watch and pray," how can you say you can do without it?

Sooner or later, in the life of every single human being, there comes a moment when we know we need to pray—a moment of personal crisis when prayer ceases to be a mere childhood habit or religious formality and becomes an emotional and spiritual lifeline. It may be, as in David's case, a situation of intense danger, a heart attack perhaps. It may be a period of devastating loss, a bereavement. It may be a moment of broken-hearted despair or humiliating guilt or paralyzing fear. However and whenever that personal crisis comes, at least one such experience comes to every one of us, when we desperately need to pray.

The question David has for us in this psalm is quite simple. When that moment comes for us, as it certainly came for him, will we know how to pray? Will we know how to cast our cares on the Lord? We can do without prayer if we insist upon it; God isn't going to force us to cast our cares on him. If we insist on living our lives in our own strength, with our own resources, he is not going to stop us. But are we so sure that our resources can cope? How do you cope with a crisis?

4

GROWING THROUGH DOUBT

*A*ll Christians at some time or another question their faith. People who tell me that isn't so are either dishonest or extremely unobservant. For anybody with a modicum of intelligence can see that there is an awful lot in this world that seems, on the face of it, to contradict a breezy confidence in God. There arc famincs and carthquakes, terminal cancer and congenital handicap. There are disasters and wars, miseries and sufferings of a thousand kinds in this world; and every honest Christian asks the same silent question: How can a good God allow it?

The only sort of faith that is immune from that kind of questioning is a blind faith, a faith that dare not look the realities of the world in the face, a faith that has to close its mind off to anything that threatens its creed. That is an irrational faith, a cowardly faith. It is a faith that fully deserves the contempt of the skeptic, for it confirms that believers are just pathetic weaklings who need a crutch of faith with which to limp through life. But real faith isn't blind. Real faith doesn't shut its eyes to evidence that seems to contradict its convictions; it can't do so. Real faith has to confront the suffering and the evil of this world. It has to accept the experience of doubt that accompanies this confrontation because failure to do so would be the denial of true faith, not an affirmation.

Perhaps that's what the poet Tennyson meant when he said that there was more faith in honest doubt than in half the creeds. Contrary to popular myth, doubt is not the opposite of faith. To suggest that it is, is to confuse doubt with unbelief; whereas doubt and unbelief are, in fact, two quite different things. If you think about it, doubt is something only a believer can experience, for you can only doubt what you believe. Doubt is to unbelief what temptation is to sin—a test, but not yet a surrender.

Psalm 73

[1]Surely God is good to Israel,
to those who are pure in heart.

[2]But as for me, my feet had almost slipped;
I had nearly lost my foothold.
[3]For I envied the arrogant
when I saw the prosperity of the wicked.

[4]They have no struggles;
their bodies are healthy and strong.
[5]They are free from the burdens common to man;
they are not plagued by human ills.
[6]Therefore pride is their necklace;
they clothe themselves with violence.
[7]From their callous hearts comes iniquity;
the evil conceits of their minds know no limits.
[8]They scoff, and speak with malice;
in their arrogance they threaten oppression.
[9]Their mouths lay claim to heaven,
and their tongues take possession of the earth.
[10]Therefore their people turn to them
and drink up waters in abundance.
[11]They say, "How can God know?
Does the Most High have knowledge?"

[12]This is what the wicked are like—
always carefree, they increase in wealth.

[13]Surely in vain have I kept my heart pure;
in vain have I washed my hands in innocence.

.¹⁴All day long I have been plagued;
 I have been punished every morning.

¹⁵If I had said, "I will speak thus,"
 I would have betrayed your children.
¹⁶When I tried to understand all this,
 it was oppressive to me
¹⁷till I entered the sanctuary of God;
 then I understood their final destiny.

¹⁸Surely you place them on slippery
 ground;
 you cast them down to ruin.
¹⁹How suddenly are they destroyed,
 completely swept away by terrors!
²⁰As a dream when one awakes,
 so when you arise, O Lord,
 you will despise them as fantasies.

²¹When my heart was grieved
 and my spirit embittered,

²²I was senseless and ignorant;
 I was a brute beast before you.

²³Yet I am always with you;
 you hold me by my right hand.
²⁴You guide me with your counsel,
 and afterward you will take me into
 glory.
²⁵Whom have I in heaven but you?
 And earth has nothing I desire besides
 you.
²⁶My flesh and my heart may fail,
 but God is the strength of my heart
 and my portion forever.
²⁷Those who are far from you will perish;
 you destroy all who are unfaithful to
 you.
²⁸But as for me, it is good to be near God.
 I have made the Sovereign LORD my
 refuge;
 I will tell of all your deeds.

What is the Book of Job if it isn't the story of a believer wrestling with doubt? Job didn't cease to be a believer during his long ordeal; on the contrary, properly understood, the very struggles he had with doubt testify to the tenacity of his faith. At the end of the day, they contributed toward the development of his faith and the strengthening of it. In fact, this is a general truth of practical Christian experience. Doubt only becomes a problem when you are afraid of it and run away from it. Christians who have the courage to engage with doubt, honestly and frankly, find that far from being weakened by the conflict, their experience of God, in fact, grows stronger and more intimate as a result of those inner struggles.

There is no better example of this in all the Bible than Psalm 73. This is the Book of Job in a nutshell. Here's a poem written by a man who knew exactly what doubt felt like. He tells us in verse 2 that he came within a hair's breadth of abandoning his faith in God altogether: "But as for me, my feet had almost slipped; I had nearly lost my foothold." Yet the testimony of this man at the end of the psalm is that he felt closer to God than ever before: "But as for me, it is good to be near God. I have made the Sovereign LORD my refuge" (v. 28). In the intervening verses, he tells us the story of a remarkable spiritual pilgrimage: how he progressed from doubt back to a full confidence in God.

The Problem Giving Rise to Doubt

We start by identifying the particular problem that gave rise to this man's doubts. Just as we've already anticipated, it arose out of the contradiction he observed between faith and reason, between theological theory and observed fact. The theological theory is stated in verse 1: "Surely God is good to Israel, to those who are pure in heart." That was his creed. I suspect he said it every Sabbath. It was the affirmation of any faithful Jew of his day. It is a nice comforting thought: God can be relied upon to be good to good people. Any Israelite who faithfully obeys the Ten Commandments can expect the Lord to honor that ancient covenant he made with Moses, and bless him, unreservedly, for his obedience. But as the psalmist looked around the world, he observed that things didn't square up with that credal position of his. If anything, the evidence was rather weighted to the contrary. He observed the prosperity, not of the pure in heart, but of the wicked. They had no struggles; their bodies were healthy and strong. They were free from the burdens common to man.

There is a note of cynicism and bitterness flowing through verses 3–11. It is as if the psalmist is saying, "Come on, let's face it, whatever we say in worship, it is the corrupt and the callous people of this world who have no problems. They get away with murder. Physically they seem to be a picture of health; emotionally they don't have any of the anxiety or depression that burden us. Proud and contemptuous as they are, they shoot their mouths off; they boss people about; but nothing ever seems to happen to humiliate them. They are ruthless and cruel; they intimidate and oppress other people; but nobody ever seems to call them to account for their crimes.

"On the contrary," he says, "as often as not, they get rewarded for their crimes with popularity. The people turn to them and drink in their words like water" (v. 10). "They admire them; they flatter them; they suck up to them. Nothing succeeds like success. These people talk like atheists. They say, 'God is an irrelevancy to us. He doesn't know anything about us; he's not going to do anything to punish us. All that hellfire and damnation is just old wives' tales; nothing bad is ever going to happen to us.' And," says the psalmist, "nothing ever does. This is what the wicked are like—always carefree. They increase in wealth" (v. 12).

This is the problem that leads to the poet's doubts. It is not so-called acts of God, like famines and tornadoes and so on, that challenged his faith. Rather it is acts of humans: injustice and exploitation and violence. How can God let them get away with it? That's his question. The Bible says that God is good to the pure in heart, but again and again, as he looks around the world, he notes the prosperity of the wicked. It is a problem with which we can all sympathize.

In recent times we have read of the appalling cases of child abuse and murder that are on police files. Many of them are unsolved. These people have gotten away with it. We hear of violent bank robbers who are living in luxury in South America on the proceeds of their crimes, writing articles in Sunday newspapers sometimes, proud of the fact that they too have gotten away with it. We hear of vicious dictators who have survived to die peacefully in their beds in spite of all the cruelty and oppression they have inflicted on other people. They have gotten away with it as well.

It's an unjust world. Virtue is triumphant only in the theater! Surely God is good to Israel, to those who are pure in heart? Pull the other leg, Moses! You'll have to make the world honest before you can honestly say that honesty is the best policy.

Perhaps we are inclined to ask, "All right, it's a problem, but what's new about it?" Surely the psalmist didn't suddenly wake up one day and notice for the first time that the wicked were doing all right. Surely that fact had been obvious to him for years? Why did it suddenly turn into a crisis of faith for this man? You'll find the answer to that in verses 13–14:

> Surely in vain have I kept my heart pure;
>   in vain have I washed my hands in innocence.
> All day long I have been plagued;
>   I have been punished every morning.

It shouldn't be so, but if we are honest we have to admit that for most of us innocent suffering remains a purely academic problem until we become the suffering innocent in question. Only then do we get bothered about it. Only then does the problem of innocent suffering begin to assume massive proportions in our minds.

It is just human nature, I am afraid. The French have a proverb: We are strong enough to bear the ills of others. Yes we are. It is our own ills that we get angry about. When an election comes, though 95 percent of the electorate will persuade themselves that they are really trying to vote for what is best for the country, the truth is they will be voting for what they perceive as best for themselves. The essayist Hazlitt wrote, "The smallest pain in my little finger generates more mental concern in me than the destruction of thousands of my fellowmen."

Still, at least the psalmist doesn't mask the fundamentally self-centered nature of his anger about the prosperity of the wicked. It would have been easy for him to have rationalized his skepticism with high-sounding cant about social injustice and the exploitation of the poor. He could have ranted and raved about the evils of the capitalist system, or about the failure of the government to maintain proper law and order. I think it is to his credit that he is honest enough to look inside his heart and confess that his moral indignation was born more of enlightened self-interest than genuine moral idealism. "I envied the arrogant," he says in verse 3. "That's the truth of the matter; I envied them. If I had shared their prosperity, I would have been a great deal less bothered about the toleration God was showing toward these wicked people. It is only when I found myself victimized by God's providence, when I found myself plagued all day long, punished every morning, that these hostile questions began to rise within me."

That's true of most of us. We read daily in our newspapers of children killed on the roads, but it never really threatens our faith until it's our child that's involved in the accident. We hear of hundreds of people in the hospital dying from cancer or heart attacks, but we never feel it to be a massive spiritual problem until it's *my* wife or *my* husband that is in the mortuary. There are thousands of unemployed people walking the streets in our country. We pass them every day, but it is not until *I* lose *my* job, that I suddenly start waving my fist at heaven and complaining about all the injustice in the world. That's the way we are. The question we always want to ask is: "Why me? There are lots of people in the world more wicked than I am, God, so why do I have to be the one to suffer? Why do I have to be the one who is poor, the one who is sick, the one who has lost my loved one? Why does it happen to me?" Those first person singulars give us away. It is not our social conscience that is really outraged; it is our envy that has been inflamed. "I envied the arrogant when I saw the prosperity of the wicked," says the psalmist.

Still, the problem he poses is a real one. Even if our motives are mixed in raising it, what answer are we to give to it? How are we to defend God against the charge of moral indifference? What remedy are we to apply to a faith that is fast slipping into despair under the assault of these kinds of doubts? Perhaps like the psalmist, we feel ourselves under attack from doubt for similar reasons. Things have gone wrong in our lives, and we do not feel we deserve it. The devil is feeding into our minds thoughts like, "You can't really believe in God if he does that to you." Maybe we feel like the psalmist: "In vain have I kept my heart pure. . . . All day long I have been plagued; I have been punished every morning."

If that is so, then this psalm ought to be of great encouragement to us. We are not unbelievers simply because we feel like that. We are not unbelievers because we want to talk to God like that. Indeed, this psalm is in the Bible to *encourage* us to talk like that. It's OK to express such thoughts. Inspired men of God in the Bible expressed the same thoughts, so why shouldn't we? We are not unbelievers because we have doubt. There is an answer to our doubt. The psalmist found it; we can too.

The Solution to Doubt

> If I had said, "I will speak thus,"
>   I would have betrayed your children.
> When I tried to understand all this,
>   it was oppressive to me
> till I entered the sanctuary of God;
>   then I understood their final destiny (73:15–17).

John Wesley recounts in his journals how one day he was walking with a friend who was very troubled with his personal trials and was expressing doubt about God's goodness. "I don't know," he said, "what I am going to do with all my doubts." Wesley pointed to a cow that was looking over a stone wall adjoining the road where they were walking. "Why do you think that cow is looking over the wall?" he asked. "Well, I suppose because she can't see through it," said his friend, rather naively. "Precisely," said Wesley. "You can't see through your doubts; you must try looking over them." He went on to explain what he meant. The advice "Look to the Lord" may sound a little glib. It is sometimes used by Christians as a rather trite platitude to avoid really getting involved with other people's problems. But rightly understood and rightly applied, it enshrines a therapy that is the answer to doubt as the psalmist here discovered. "It was oppressive to me," he sang, "till I entered the sanctuary of God."

We human beings are like the moon: we live on borrowed light. When our faces are turned away from God, we are always left with nothing but the darkness of our own shadows. The first step out of doubt is always to turn our eyes from the problem to catch a glimpse of God himself. That is what happened to the psalmist. He was so battered by the perplexity of his mental and emotional struggle that he tells us he was within an ace of abandoning worship altogether. Thoughts were going through his head that, if he had actually vocalized them publicly, would have constituted blasphemy and apostasy. "If I had said what was in my mind," he says, "I would have betrayed your people."

Yet somehow in the midst of this spiritual turmoil, he found his way to the temple. Maybe he couldn't avoid going; perhaps he was in the choir or had to preach! Anyhow, it was there that at last his mind began to clear. What did he discover there in the sanctuary that so transformed his attitude to his doubt? He discovered new perspectives on three things: on human destiny, on himself, and on real values.

A New Perspective on Human Destiny

> then I understood their final destiny.
>
> Surely you placed them on slippery ground;
>   you cast them down to ruin (73:17b–18).

One of the things that worship does, indeed the *primary* thing that worship does, is to put God at the center of our vision. Worship is an exercise in theocentric thinking. And it is vitally important because it is only when God is at the center of our vision that we see things as they really are. So long as we put ourselves at the center, our vision of life is out of proportion; we don't see things in their true perspective. Worship delivers us from that distorting self-absorption. It enables us to see things in God's light. When we cannot see through our doubts, worship enables us to see over them.

The psalmist was bothered because wicked people seemed to be doing rather well. It wasn't until he started to worship that he suddenly realized he wasn't seeing things from the perspective of God at all; he was seeing things from the short-sighted perspective of a time-bound observer. Once he got these wicked men in heaven's perspective, their destiny looked altogether different. "Then I understood their final destiny," he says. "Surely you placed them on slippery ground."

The trouble with us human beings is that we tend to ignore what we can't see. The future is unknown to us, so we live as if it didn't exist. We live for today. God's response to that sort of preoccupation with the present moment is always to say, "You are foolish. Your soul is going to be required of you one day. What does it profit a man if he gains the whole world and loses his soul?" I know people mock talk of judgment and the end of the world; but the fact is, as far as the Bible is concerned, these things are dreadfully real. If they weren't real, there would be no hope for goodness in this world. There would be no real reason for pursuing goodness, because in the final analysis, goodness wouldn't count for anything. It is only because the God who made this world intends to give his moral verdict on human history at its end that we dare to believe that goodness matters. Without judgment, God and the world are reduced to moral indifference.

The person of faith is one who, because he has God's perspective on history, takes the future seriously. Like Moses, he is content, if necessary, to share ill treatment with the people of God, rather than to continue to enjoy the temporary pleasures of being a member of Pharaoh's court. He is looking to the long term. He knows what counts in the final analysis. People who haven't got that perception of the future, inevitably, will see no real value in goodness. You have to believe it counts, long term, to be committed to goodness, because in the short term there are many sufferings for good people. That is the reality of the world.

The person of faith realizes that just because the future cannot be seen does not mean it is imaginary. God sees it, even though we don't. His reality includes tomorrow as well as today. The psalmist points out that from God's perspective, the prosperity of the wicked is as illusory as a dream.

> As a dream when one awakes,
>> so when you arise, O Lord,
>> you will despise them as fantasies (73:20).

Have you ever had one of those nightmares where you wake up suddenly, and you are sweating with anxiety? You switch the bedroom light on, and suddenly you laugh at your foolishness. It all seemed so real, but it wasn't. Once you wake up, you despise it as an illusion and think no more about it. "What a fool I was," you say, "to get so excited about a dream." That's how God sees the prosperity of the wicked. It is not real because it is not eternal. One day we shall awake and realize that kind of prosperity is an insubstantial figment of the imagination. Indeed, perhaps there is no more terrible judgment upon such wickedness of men, than that on the last day they will find themselves finally and unspeakably ignored. "Depart from me, I never knew you," Jesus will say. "You are not real; you are not part of my eternity." What a terrifying prospect—to be despised by God as an unpleasant nightmare.

Once he went into the temple and put God in the center of the stage, the psalmist was able to see just how precarious was this prosperity of godless men that he was envying so much.

A New Perspective on Ourselves

> When my heart was grieved
>> and my spirit embittered,
> I was senseless and ignorant;
>> I was a brute beast before you.
>
> Yet I am always with you;
>> you hold me by my right hand.
> You guide me with your counsel,
>> and afterward you will take me into glory (73:21–24).

Part of our trouble is that once we get into a mood of morbid introspection, it very quickly becomes a vicious circle. We do not feel like worshiping God; we would rather wallow in our self-pity and nourish our resentment against him. So we lock ourselves away securely in the prison of our own self-absorption, and the darkness grows deeper and deeper. That's what always happens in our doubting times. Perhaps that's one reason why a *habit* of coming to church on Sundays is a good thing. If we didn't discipline ourselves to worship God regularly and thus put him in the center of our lives, then when doubts and problems came, we would not have the help of the vital heavenly perspective that only worship can give to us. A good habit will often overrule a weak will and save us from untold misery in this regard; because once we are in the place of worship, willingly or not, we are exposed to the presence of God. As soon as we open up our hearts to God's presence, we see ourselves as we really are. We see things about ourselves that we would perhaps rather not see.

We see, for instance, the sulkiness of our behavior; we see the childishness of our resentment. We see how pathetic our self-pity is: "I envied the arrogant." Yes, we are able even to be honest enough to admit that envy is really what it came down to. And we kick ourselves with embarrassment for entertaining such foolish attitudes: "When my heart was grieved and my spirit embittered, I was senseless and ignorant; I was a brute beast before you."

When the psalmist came to the place of worship, he found that he could put his bitterness, his senselessness, and his brutishness behind him. What's more, he suddenly discovered something else about himself. He suddenly discovered that in spite of all his doubts and foolish talk, he nevertheless was a child of God.

> Yet I am always with you;
>   you hold me by my right hand.
> You guide me with your counsel,
>   and afterward you will take me into glory (73:23–24).

So long as we stay away from church, we can hide from this truth about ourselves. The devil can tell us: "You're not a real Christian. How can you be a Christian? Thinking the way you do about God, angry as you are with God? Having all these doubts? You—a Christian? Don't make me laugh!" It isn't until we come into the experience of worship and put God at the center of the stage, that we realize it is not only our doubts we have to come to terms with; it is our faith, too. Our experience of God is just as much a real part of our lives as these doubts that trouble us.

Circumstances may arise that we find extremely difficult to reconcile intellectually with the reality of God. But no amount of circumstances can annihilate that reality. One of the reasons we come into God's house every week is to rediscover, through worship, this fundamental truth about ourselves: that God is always with us, that he holds us by our right hand, that he guides us with his counsel, that he will take us to glory.

To surrender to our doubts would be just as false to our true selves as if we pretended those doubts didn't exist. It is very important to grasp hold of this. Faith is not a delicate little plant that we have to keep in a greenhouse for fear that it is going to get knocked down by the wind and the rain. Faith is a hardy perennial; it can stand the bad weather. For faith isn't something we have concocted out of our own feelings, nor is it a carefully proven thesis of human logic that we have decided we agree with. Faith is an intuitive grasp of spiritual reality; it is a supernatural assurance that springs up even when everything around it seems guaranteed to extinguish it—even when we ourselves, perhaps, try to extinguish it. If you don't believe that's true, you just try the sort of experiment the psalmist here conducted.

Say to yourself, "I am fed up with Christianity! I have far too many intellectual problems to be a Christian any longer. I am going to give it up. I'm going to throw in the towel." Try it! You will discover, as the psalmist did, that no sooner have you conducted such an experiment, than you realize it is impossible. You can't give up faith in that fashion, for it doesn't adhere in the personality like that. As hard as we try to deny it, true faith keeps reasserting itself. Like a cork pushed down under the surface of water, you only have to lift your finger and up it bobs again. Faith is not something we cook up in ourselves. It is not sustained by our willpower. It is something God has put into our souls. We can no more run away from it than we can run away from our own heartbeat.

The psalmist discovered that about himself in the temple. While he stayed out of contact with God, he could kid himself that he wasn't a believer. He could live as if he wasn't a believer, and it wouldn't make any difference. But as soon as he was brought face to face with God in worship, the illusion dissolved. "What a fool I am," he said. "It was just the bitterness of my heart that was making me think I could possibly be like that. Now I realize, 'I am always with you; you hold me by my right hand. You guide me with your counsel . . . you will take me into glory.'"

A New Perspective on Real Values

> Whom have I in heaven but you?
>   And earth has nothing I desire besides you.
> My flesh and my heart may fail,
>   but God is the strength of my heart
>   and my portion forever (73:25–26).

Professor Joad became famous because whenever he was asked a question as a radio panelist, he always started his answer with the words: "Well, it all depends on what you mean by . . ." I guess if we were asked to comment on the question, "Is God good to the pure in heart?" we might be similarly justified in replying, "Well, it all depends on what you mean by *good.*" If you mean, "Does God make all pure in heart people rich?" then it is palpably not true. If you mean, "Does God make all pure in heart people healthy?" that is not true either. If you mean, "Does God make all pure in heart people popular?" that too isn't true. So if bestowing health, riches, and popularity is what you mean by doing people good, God is not good to the pure in heart. But then those kinds of benefits, though they may be real blessings in their way, are not what real goodness consists of. Indeed, it is the tragedy of many people in this world that they allow the pursuit of such good things to rob them of the best things.

> Whom have I in heaven but you?
>   And earth has nothing I desire besides you (73:25).

Some of us, in the enthusiastic flush of young romance, held somebody's hand and said, "For richer, for poorer; in sickness and in health;

for better, for worse." If we meant those promises, then we were saying that having that person in our lives is more precious to us than any other good thing we can think of. The very enjoyment of what prosperity we have in life depends on our ability to share it with them. Being with them, we really desire nothing else. If human love can be such a precious treasure, if it can make us so indifferent to materialistic or physical welfare, then where should the love of God figure in our scale of values? "My flesh and my heart may fail," writes the psalmist, "but God is the strength of my heart and my portion forever."

Someday we may have paid off our mortgages, but the house will still fall down eventually. One of these days we may get that car we have been longing for, but it will still rust. Do we really believe that those are the things that make life good? No, here is the pearl of great price for which a man sells all he has. The psalmist discovered the beauty of that pearl when he came into God's house to worship, and in the light of that beauty, his envy at the prosperity of others dissolved away. He got things back in perspective. "Yes, God is good to Israel," he says, "but I am going to define what I mean by 'good.' As for me, it is good to be near God; that is what I mean by 'good.' Being with him, I desire nothing else on earth."

Here it is, then, a man with doubts who struggles his way through to become a man with a testimony. Maybe you are the academic type and your doubts arise from your intellectual discipline. You have problems with the inspiration of the Bible, or with miracles, or something of that sort. Maybe you are an unsophisticated person. You don't have any pretensions of being academic, and your doubts tend to arise more from the practical sufferings and injustices of life. Whatever the source of your doubts is, don't run away from them. All that the Christian who closes his mind to a subject or an issue that threatens his faith is actually confessing is his unbelief. For if he really believed his religion was true, he could launch into any sphere of human inquiry, any experience of human life, in the confidence that the truth would vindicate itself. We must not allow ourselves to yield to the schoolboy definition of faith: Faith is believing what you know ain't true. That is nonsense. Compelling myself to believe is no part of true religion; a Christian believes under the constraint of the Truth. Jesus said, "I am the Truth." We don't give up the quest for truth and receive Jesus instead. It is as the Truth that Jesus wants to be received. He is more concerned than anybody else about our integrity. A profession of faith achieved only by jettisoning that integrity doesn't please him.

There is nothing unspiritual about doubts. Learn that from the psalmist. Great saints of God have struggled with doubt. What is unspiritual is to refuse to acknowledge doubt, to hide from it, to pretend it's not there. All that policy will do in the long run is to weaken your faith, just like a muscle that wastes away from lack of use because its owner is forever fearful of straining it. Instead, look doubt in the face. Maybe you will have to struggle as the psalmist did; maybe you will have to shed tears as he did; but in the long run, the reality of God in your life will be stronger, not weaker, because you have wrestled with doubts in that way.

The answer to doubt is not to be less honest with yourself, but to be more honest with yourself—honest with yourself about the questions you have, but honest with yourself also about that irrepressible, irresistible seed of faith that keeps on tugging at your mind and heart and demanding that you recognize it. Isn't it time you stopped complaining about doubts and started surrendering to your faith? Isn't it time you passed from the agony of all those questions you cannot answer, to the challenge of that truth that deep in your heart you know you cannot deny?

5

DISCOVERING GOD IN SICKNESS

*I*t is quite clear that many modern men and women are absolutely obsessed with health. The evidence for that obsession is everywhere: early morning joggers reduce their risk of heart disease and increase their risk of osteoarthritis; supermarkets eliminate the dangers posed by food additives and increase the dangers posed by salmonella poisoning. In every magazine medical insurance plans are advertised. There are enough bottles of pills and tablets piled high in every pharmacy store to satisfy the appetites of a whole army of hypochondriacs. Then there are hospitals: lavish temples dedicated to our twentieth century gods of healing, with their thousands of white-coated priests, ministering the sacraments of modern medicine.

People today take their health very seriously indeed. Yet in spite of all the advances that our century has seen in the cure and the prevention of disease, ironically, people at the end of the twentieth century are more afraid of becoming sick than ever before. The sixteenth century playwright Thomas Nashe wrote a poem during the time that the bubonic plague troubled Elizabethan England. It may not be a brilliant poem, but it is interesting because of the attitude it expresses toward illness. Here are just three of the stanzas:

> Adieu, farewell Earth's bliss,
> This world uncertain is.
> Fond are life's lustful joys,
> Death proves them all but toys.
> None from his darts can fly,
> I am sick, I must die.
> Lord, have mercy on us.
>
> Rich men trust not in wealth,
> Gold cannot buy you health.
> Medicine itself must fade,
> All things to end, are made.
> The plague, full swift, goes by,
> I am sick, I must die.
> Lord, have mercy on us.
>
> Haste, therefore, each degree
> To welcome destiny.
> Heaven is our heritage,
> Earth but a players' stage.
> Mount we unto the sky,
> I am sick, I must die.
> Lord, have mercy on us.

It is hard to imagine any twentieth century poet expressing that kind of attitude in the face of illness. Today sickness is seen to be an illegitimate intruder. We expect to be healthy; we have a right to be healthy. Illness, even incurable terminal illness, is an enemy that we rage against to our last breath. It doesn't matter how radical the surgery, how devastating the chemotherapy, one just does not accept illness today in the way that Thomas Nashe seems to do in his poem. It is not so much a case of "I am sick, I must die. Lord, have mercy on us," but, "I am sick and I must *not* die. Doctor, you must do something." And in a subtle way that refusal to come to terms with illness, which is characteristic of our culture, has manifested itself in Christian circles too. It is interesting that as the secular world has become increasingly obsessed with health, so the church has become ever more obsessed with healing. The two things have gone in tandem.

Of course, there has always been, especially in the Roman Catholic tradition, an interest in miraculous cures, epitomized by the popularity of pilgrimages to that grotto at Lourdes where Bernadette is supposed to have seen the Virgin Mary. Unfortunately, there is a great deal of superstition in that particular kind of quest for healing.

At the other extreme, but equally unconvincing, are the followers of Mary Baker Eddy, the founder of the Christian Scientists, a movement that on closer observation, proves to be neither Christian nor very scientific. Christian Science says that illness is all in the mind. Mrs. Eddy, for instance, in her book, *Science and Health*, at one point has this extraordinary sentence: "A boil simply manifests through inflammation and swelling, a person's belief in pain. The belief is called a 'boil.'" The implication is that if only you convince yourself the pain doesn't exist, the boil will disappear. There is a famous limerick which justly parodies that nonsense:

> There was a faith-healer from Deal
> Who said that though pain is not real,
> When I sit on a pin
> And it punctures my skin,
> I dislike what I fancy I feel.

Notwithstanding these extremes of superstition and fanaticism that have always been around in Christian circles, it has to be said that there is today a growing movement within mainstream, evangelical Christianity that wishes to put supernatural, divine healing high on the church's agenda. Various streams of argument flow into that new interest. Some see it simply as a following of the example of Jesus, who went about healing and, on one occasion at least, told his disciples to do the same. Some see it as a theological consequence of the atonement. They make much of that verse in Isaiah 53: "Surely he has borne our infirmities and carried our sicknesses." Illness, they argue, is a consequence of sin; and since Jesus has borne our sins on the cross, he must also have potentially acquired physical healing for us. Most recently, writers like John Wimber have stressed the role of healing as a visible sign of God's power over evil, without which he says our evangelism lacks credibility.

One thing all these contemporary advocates of healing are agreed upon is that a Christian ought not to surrender to illness meekly. Any kind of resignation, they say, is out of place. A Christian ought to expect deliverance from sickness and, in that regard, Thomas Nashe's poem betrays a culpable lack of faith. A Christian, they say, shouldn't pray, "I am sick, I must die. Lord, have mercy on us." That is far too defeatist. Rather a Christian should pray something like this: "I am sick but I won't die. Lord, I claim healing in Jesus' name."

I want to issue a gentle caution about that kind of praying. I don't want to be misunderstood in this: I believe that God does heal people in ways that defy medical explanation, and I am personally grateful for those who issue regular reminders to us that we should not be so brainwashed by the antisupernaturalism and the skepticism of our secular age that we are not open to those miraculous interventions of God into our lives. I have to say, however, that I do not believe that miraculous healing is taking place with anything like the frequency which some Christians seem to be implying. Indeed, I believe such incidents, ever since the end of the Apostolic Age, have always been rather rare in the church. I find it mischievous and not a little irresponsible for people to create an atmosphere of expectation that it can be otherwise, because an atmosphere like that inevitably leads to disillusionment of a most cruel kind.

Some years ago a report was published of a young woman in Brighton whose baby died after being delivered without any medical assistance. The woman belonged to a Christian group who were very keen on healing, and she had been told that she could claim a supernatural delivery for her child. The woman's verdict, after the baby's death, was, "I didn't have enough faith. There was a fault in me which let in the devil." One American newspaper, which ran an article about a particularly extremist healer, claims that fifty-two people have died as a direct consequence of this man's teaching in the last few years. More recently a BBC investigation into the results of Morris Cerullo's London healing crusade found it impossible to discover an unambiguous example of supernatural healing in spite of extravagant media claims. In my own pastoral ministry I have had to deal with people who are confused and bewildered as a result of expected healing that did not occur. They feel that somehow they are to blame; they haven't had enough faith; some sin in them is stopping the power. Many of us, I guess, were first awakened to this by the controversy over the death of David Watson, a prominent Anglican evangelical, greatly used by God. It was said by certain people in this modern healing school, "He's not going to die; he's going to be healed." They insisted that we should all believe it. But David Watson died of cancer.

At the risk of being written off by some, I have to share my personal conviction that much of this Christian obsession with healing is just a religious echo of that secular obsession with health with which this chapter began. Far from being a sign of spiritual renewal, I regard this preoccupation with spiritual healing as a sign of worldliness in the church. It is one more evidence of the way narcissistic twentieth-century people think they have a right to good health and will go to any lengths to evade the reality of their own mortality and frailty. Because they think that they have a right to healing, they will twist their minds into all kinds of double-think in order to evade the fact that miraculous healing is, in fact, a very rare event.

The people of God still get sick and die. Indeed, I would suggest that Thomas Nashe's poem, for all its poetic inadequacy, expresses something that is closer to the biblical attitude to illness than many Christians today might think. His poem comes close to the spirit and attitude of the psalmist in Psalm 102.

The Prayer of an Afflicted Man

If you look at the heading of this psalm, you will see that it is subtitled "The prayer of an afflicted man. When he is faint and pours out his lament before the LORD." Judging from one or two things he says during his lament, his afflictions may have been compounded of more than one element. In verse 8, for instance, he talks about enemies taunting him. In verse 14 his reference to his fondness for the dust and the stones of Zion suggests that he may well have been one of those taken into exile by the Babylonian enemy. The allusion to the groaning of prisoners in verse 20 may be a personal reference too. It is far from unlikely that this man may have been in a prisoner-of-war camp or something similar, after the destruction of Jerusalem. However, what is unquestionable is that whatever his situation may have exactly been, the man who writes this psalm is ill, for he describes his illness in graphic detail in verses 3–11.

Psalm 102

¹Hear my prayer, O LORD;
  let my cry for help come to you.
²Do not hide your face from me
  when I am in distress.
Turn your ear to me;
  when I call, answer me quickly.

³For my days vanish like smoke;
  my bones burn like glowing embers.
⁴My heart is blighted and withered like
    grass;
  I forget to eat my food.
⁵Because of my loud groaning
  I am reduced to skin and bones.
⁶I am like a desert owl,
  like an owl among the ruins.
⁷I lie awake; I have become
  like a bird alone on a roof.
⁸All day long my enemies taunt me;
  those who rail against me use my
    name as a curse.
⁹For I eat ashes as my food
  and mingle my drink with tears
¹⁰because of your great wrath,

for you have taken me up and thrown
    me aside.
¹¹My days are like the evening shadow;
  I wither away like grass.

¹²But you, O LORD, sit enthroned forever;
  your renown endures through all
    generations.
¹³You will arise and have compassion on
    Zion,
  for it is time to show favor to her;
  the appointed time has come.
¹⁴For her stones are dear to your servants;
  her very dust moves them to pity.
¹⁵The nations will fear the name of the
    LORD,
  all the kings of the earth will revere
    your glory.
¹⁶For the LORD will rebuild Zion
  and appear in his glory.
¹⁷He will respond to the prayer of the
    destitute;
  he will not despise their plea.

¹⁸Let this be written for a future
    generation,

that a people not yet created may praise the LORD:

¹⁹"The LORD looked down from his sanctuary on high,
from heaven he viewed the earth,
²⁰to hear the groans of the prisoners
and release those condemned to death."
²¹So the name of the LORD will be declared in Zion
and his praise in Jerusalem
²²when the peoples and the kingdoms assemble to worship the LORD.

²³In the course of my life he broke my strength;
he cut short my days.
²⁴So I said:

"Do not take me away, O my God, in the midst of my days;
your years go on through all generations.
²⁵In the beginning you laid the foundations of the earth,
and the heavens are the work of your hands.
²⁶They will perish, but you remain;
they will all wear out like a garment.
Like clothing you will change them
and they will be discarded.
²⁷But you remain the same,
and your years will never end.
²⁸The children of your servants will live in your presence;
their descendants will be established before you."

Clearly it had been a long illness. He speaks about his days having vanished like smoke. Perhaps he was thinking of all those things he had wanted to do with his time but had had to abandon. All his plans had disappeared into thin air. It also seems to have been an acute illness. He speaks about his bones burning like glowing embers, which is probably a reference either to the high temperature he was suffering, or perhaps to the intensity of his pain.

As is so often the case with illness, it left him feeling exhausted, his inner resources utterly spent. "My heart is blighted and withered like grass." His appetite had disappeared. "I forget to eat my food," he says. So it wasn't surprising that he had lost an awful lot of weight. "Because of my loud groaning I am reduced to skin and bones." Anyone who has experienced serious illness will empathize with all this. They will empathize, too, with the sense of isolation he feels, stuck in his bed, flat on his back for twenty-four hours a day. He likens himself in verse 6 to a solitary bird of prey, perched amidst the deserted and devastated city, sleepless and lonely, with the night passing so slowly. "I am like a desert owl," he says, "like an owl among the ruins. I lie awake; I have become like a bird alone on a roof."

When daylight does dawn, to make matters worse, there are those enemies of his who extract smug satisfaction from his plight. "They rail against me; they taunt me," he says. "They use my name as a curse." Not surprisingly, the strain of it all eventually begins to wear down his emotional as well as his physical resistance: "I eat ashes as my food and mingle my drink with tears," he says. In the ancient world ashes were a symbol of grief, but this man felt as if he were not pouring ashes on his head as a mourner normally would; he was suffering the additional humiliation of being forced to eat ashes too, as his daily diet. "No joy for me," he says, "sorrow and pain is all I feel."

He complains, in verse 10, that it is God's fault: "because of your great wrath, for you have taken me up and thrown me aside." It is as if God had contemptuously tossed him aside like a child throwing a toy out of a stroller. He has little hope of recovery; the illness seems to have all the signs of being a terminal condition. "The light is fading," he says, "life is slowly ebbing away." He feels that he already has one foot in the grave. "My days are like the evening shadow; I wither away like grass." It is a very candid expression of how a man feels under the assault of an acute illness.

How are we to react to such words? I suspect that quite a few Christians today would be rather dissatisfied with them. They would feel that there was too much self-pity, too much defeatism, and not enough confidence, not enough victory in them. The psalmist is behaving as though it were God's will for him to be ill, as if God had decreed this affliction and there was nothing he could do about it except resign himself to it. Like Thomas Nashe in that poem, "I am sick, I must die. Lord, have mercy on us." That's exactly his mood. Surely Jesus would have said to this man, just as he said to the troubled disciples during the storm on Galilee, "Where is your faith?" Why doesn't he claim healing?

If that is our response to the psalmist, it shows just how little understanding of real spirituality we have, and how much we have been brainwashed by the contemporary obsession with health. This is a man of great faith; this whole psalm is a psalm of great faith. If you don't believe so, just observe how suddenly the tone brightens at verse 12. The whole atmosphere of the psalm lifts, because at this point the psalmist has begun to direct his thoughts toward the object of his faith. But take special note that the object of faith is not healing, it is God. A believer is not a person who believes in healing; a believer is a person who believes in God. That is what this man fastens his mind around; he sets his sickness in the context of his knowledge of God.

God's Eternal Nature

> My days are like the evening shadow;
> I wither away like grass.
>
> But you, O LORD, sit enthroned forever;
> your renown endures through all generations (102:11–12).

So the psalmist sets the transience and the fragility of his own weakness against the timelessness, the immutability, and the strength of the everlasting God. If there were any doubt of the importance of this to him, he develops it again in verses 25–27:

> In the beginning you laid the foundations of the earth,
> and the heavens are the work of your hands.
> They will perish, but you remain;
> they will all wear out like a garment.
> Like clothing you will change them
> and they will be discarded.
> But you remain the same,
> and your years will never end.

In the whole of the Old Testament there are few passages that celebrate the eternal nature of God's person with greater eloquence and grandeur. His poetry challenges the cosmology of the twentieth century just as much as it must have been a rebuke to the Babylonian mythology of his enemies. "Look back," he says, "through time. Look back as far as you can. Look back to that momentous millisecond when the whole universe began. God was there. The mathematics of the Big Bang are no mystery to him. He solved the unified field equations long ago; in fact, he encompassed their solution in the infinite scope of his own creative command. He 'laid the foundations of the earth, and the heavens are the work of [his] hands.'

87

Now look forward, look forward as far as you can into the future. Look forward to that catastrophic moment when the universe will fall apart. God will be there too. He will control the dissolution of the elements as masterfully as he controlled their creation. Like a tailor fashioning a suit of clothes, so God has sewed the universe together. Like all clothes, it is prone to decay; a day will come when the cosmos will wear out, become threadbare, and waste away. But," says the psalmist, "God the heavenly tailor won't be taken by surprise; he will transform the old worn-out world into a new world, as easily as changing a jacket on a customer. 'Like clothing you will change them and they will be discarded. But you remain the same, and your years will never end.'"

It is not difficult to see why such thoughts proved so relevant for this man to ponder in his prayer time, when he was sick. He himself was feeling worn out: "My body is tired and sick; it is exhausted. Why is it so vulnerable to frailty and weakness?" Because it is part of a universe that is wearing out, that's why. There is no escape from the ravages of time for us human beings. Our human existence is bound up with a decaying universe that is wearing out like a garment. We are essentially impermanent, ephemeral, dying. But the psalmist responds to that by placing his human mortality against the background of God's unchanging, immutable existence.

God's Eternal Purpose

> You will arise and have compassion on Zion,
>> for it is time to show favor to her;
>> the appointed time has come (102:13).

God, the sovereign Master of Time, has a special purpose for his own people. The psalmist refers to "the appointed time," the day of grace as we might call it, when the people of God will experience God's blessing in an unprecedented manner. It doesn't take much to imagine how appealing that thought would be to Jews in exile, suffering nostalgia for Jerusalem:

> For her stones are dear to your servants;
>> her very dust moves them to pity (102:14).

88

But it is clear that the psalmist is not talking about a divine purpose that is narrowly ethnocentric:

> The nations will fear the name of the LORD,
>> all the kings of the earth will revere your glory.
> For the LORD will rebuild Zion
>> and appear in his glory (102:15–16).

So he is talking about a momentous day of revelation when God will appear on earth, rather as he had done in the days of Moses. When that day arrives, the people of God will be reconstituted and supplemented by a vast international multitude of new believers. It is a magnificent vision.

What exactly is the psalmist predicting? He is predicting us! The church is the fulfillment of what he is describing in verses 13–16. This is a messianic psalm that looks forward to the coming of Jesus. If you are uncertain about that, you only have to turn to Hebrews 1 and see the way the New Testament writer quotes extensively from the words of this psalm to demonstrate the deity of Jesus. "Jesus," he says, "is that Lord of whom Psalm 102 speaks."

At the moment of its composition, that Christian fulfillment of this messianic hope still lay at least five centuries ahead. But the psalmist has no difficulty with that; he knows it is the distant future he is anticipating.

> Let this be written for a future generation,
>> that a people not yet created may praise the LORD (102:18).

But interestingly, though it is for him a distant horizon, he gains a great deal of personal comfort and satisfaction from this prospect of a future day. It gives him encouragement to pray with confidence in spite of his immediate distress:

> He will respond to the prayer of the destitute;
>> he will not despise their plea (102:17).

In fact, in verse 18, he seems to have actually composed a little anticipatory song to be sung by that new messianic community on the day that the Lord eventually arrives. He gives us the words in verse 19:

> The LORD looked down from his sanctuary on high,
>> from heaven he viewed the earth,
> to hear the groans of the prisoners
>> and release those condemned to death (102:19–20).

So he says the name of the Lord will be declared in Jerusalem when the peoples and the kingdoms assemble to worship the Lord. It rather pleases him to think that they will have a song from his pen, which they will be able to sing when they are all gathered there to praise the Lord.

Again, it is not difficult to see the relevance of this to the sick psalmist. There he was, facing death. But he finds relief from his distress in the fulfillment of God's purposes for his people. His prayers and his praises wouldn't be wasted in the long term; healing would come for the people of God as a whole, even though they would have to wait for it. That is the significance of verse 28:

> The children of your servants will live in your presence;
>> their descendants will be established before you.

He is speaking here in a typically Old Testament way about his hope for the future being in his posterity. He does not seem, in this psalm, to express any hope of personal immortality. But we live today in the light of the resurrection; we know so much more than this man did, for Jesus has come. There is a hope for us as individuals when we die; there is life beyond the grave, eternal life. So it is not just in our children that our hope is invested; we have a personal hope.

Our Response to Weakness

Should we write this psalm off as anachronistic then? Do Christians see the problem of sickness in a completely different way from the psalmist? No, that isn't so at all. In spite of the fact that he lived before Jesus, and we live after Jesus, the response that this man makes to his weakness, in the light of God's eternal nature and eternal purpose, is totally appropriate to us as Christians.

We can learn three things about prayer in time of sickness from this man's example.

Pray Honestly

> For I eat ashes as my food
>   and mingle my drink with tears
> because of your great wrath,
>   for you have taken me up and thrown me aside.
> My days are like the evening shadow;
>   I wither away like grass (102:9–11).

This is not an invalid whining to his hospital visitors. This is a man talking to God. The spontaneous reaction of this man in his sickness is to pray. As we saw in earlier chapters, what makes the believer different in times of negative experience is not that he is immune to stress, but that he has a resource the unbeliever doesn't have. He can pray. He is as vulnerable to emotional conflict as the unbeliever, but he can talk to God about that conflict. In that prayer there are no holds barred. There are no polite conventions that have to be maintained.

Once again the psalmist demonstrates uninhibited freedom in saying just what is on his mind to God, even when he feels angry and complaining. It is so important that we should be able to pray without pretending. One of the things that the obsession with healing does is to encourage an attitude of pretense in people. They are forever trying to project an image of triumphant victory and confidence in God, and the result is they never really say what is on their hearts. They put on a show of what they think a Christian under affliction ought to be like. God doesn't expect that of us.

Prayer is a relationship with God. It involves believers and God talking to one another honestly. Very often the reason that God brings negative experiences into our lives is to enhance that mutual sharing, to draw us into a closer relationship with him. Samuel Rutherford, a great saint of the Scottish church, once said: "It's a blessed fever that brings Christ to the bedside." Many of the greatest saints will tell you that their most enriching spiritual times have been their times of sickness.

This is a vital lesson that this psalm has to teach us. When we are sick, we must talk to God about it. We must be frank and candid with him. What marks a believer out is not the certainty with which he claims healing. It is his humble confidence that he can share his experience with God, knowing that God is there and listens. We need to emulate this kind of prayer, not disparage it.

Pray Humbly

> In the course of my life he broke my strength;
>> he cut short my days.
> So I said:
>> "Do not take me away, O my God, in the midst of my days;
>> your years go on through all generations" (102:23–24).

I find just a hint of humor in these verses. There is almost a tongue-in-cheek feeling in them. He is saying, "It's all right for you, God; you have all eternity to play with! I've only got a few years on this planet. Please don't terminate my life prematurely then." In that sense this is a prayer for healing. The psalmist clearly doesn't think there is any virtue in stoically putting up with his affliction; he finds it a trial, and he would like to be free of it. He would like to go on living a few more years.

However, unlike some prayer for healing that is advocated today, there is no hint of impudent demanding in this prayer. There is no suggestion that he has a right to healing and that he can claim it. It is a very humble petition. He feels his insignificance before this eternal God with his vast purposes. How could he pray other than humbly? He realized, as did Nashe, that mortal creatures like us can only pray, "Lord, have mercy on us." Such humble praying in a situation of sickness is still very much a prayer of faith.

Sadly, there are many Christians today who have such a mercenary conception of believing prayer that they see it basically as a means of getting things. It is a technique of divine manipulation: I have faith, Lord, that you are going to heal me. I thank you in advance, Lord, that you are going to do this. Such prayers sound as if believing prayer were a kind of armlock on God. But that isn't prayer at all. It is close to a form of magic. It is an attempt to control supernatural powers to do my will. It turns the Christian *Amen* into something not much less than *Abracadabra!*

Real believing prayer is about a personal relationship with God, a relationship of such trust and intimacy that life is experienced not

92

as a soliloquy, but as a dialogue. It is not about getting things; it is about sharing things.

Let me give a very powerful example: Jesus in the Garden of Gethsemane. "My Father, if it is possible," he says, "may this cup be taken from me. Yet not as I will, but as you will." Do you think it was for a lack of faith on Jesus' part that he adds that clause, "Yet not as I will, but as you will"? Is it a cop-out, in case his prayer wasn't answered? Certainly not! Christian prayer is not about manipulating God, but about surrendering to him. Prayer is not about the selfish completion of a blank check that God has pledged to sign; prayer is my acceptance of the check God has completed on my behalf. It is not a sort of magic spell; prayer is a participation in God's purposes. It is not the enforcement of my purpose on him; it is a sharing of my life with him.

Pray without pretending then! What makes a believer a believer is not the certainty with which he claims healing, but the trust he has in God's care for him.

Pray Patiently

> Let this be written for a future generation,
> that a people not yet created may praise the LORD (102:18).

That interesting phrase *not yet* occurs also in the New Testament. John wrote: "We are the children of God, now, but what we will be is *not yet* made known." Paul wrote: "We have the firstfruits of the Holy Spirit in our lives now, but we wait for the redemption of our body. In this hope, we are saved. Who hopes for what he already has, but we are hoping for what we do *not yet* have, and so we wait for it patiently."

This is a tension we have to live with, and it is most important that we get it balanced. As Christians we know the expectation of the psalmist has been fulfilled in Christ: the appointed time has come, for the Lord's glory has been seen in Zion, in Jesus. Yet there is another sense in which, just like the psalmist, we are still waiting. It is true that the seeds of the kingdom have been placed in our personalities, but that renewal is *not yet* complete. This world has *not yet* been dressed in new clothes. These bodies of ours have *not yet* been renewed; they still belong to the realm of death and sin. That is why

93

Christians are vulnerable to sickness. It is a consequence of the *not yet*. Although we are God's children now, we still wait for the redemption of our bodies.

Many in healing ministry in the church simply do not take that *not yet* seriously enough. They behave and pray as if heaven were already here. They claim now what God has promised only for the future. That is why they are so easily disillusioned. Of course a day will come when these tired, old bodies of ours with all their vulnerability to sickness will be perfectly restored, and the ravages of illness will be done away with. Then every tear will be wiped from our eyes. But it is *not yet*. So even though we are New Testament Christians, we are called in sickness to demonstrate precisely the same kind of patient faith that this Old Testament saint demonstrated. God may have mercy and heal; we can pray that he will, humbly appealing that this timeless Lord will have pity on such feeble creatures of time as we are. But we have no title to such healing, *not yet*. We have no need to feel disillusioned if healing doesn't happen. For biblical faith is anchored in the future purpose of God for his people, a people not yet created, who will praise the Lord, free from all the frustrations and limitations of this present mortality.

When you go through a time of sickness, then, pray honestly. Tell God what you are really feeling about what you are experiencing. Don't fear that you have to put up some kind of image of triumph and victory through sickness. Pray humbly, too. Of course you will want to ask for healing, but pray for it like one who is begging the Lord of heaven for a favor, not like one who is pinning God's arm behind his back. And pray patiently. Healing may not come. There is not a word in the Bible that suggests that it must come. Try not to be obsessed, then, with healing; leave that to the unbelievers who have no eternal hope. There are some things that we do *not yet* have. Don't worry— it will be worth the wait.

Part 2

SONGS IN THE DAY

6

THE PROOF OF THE PUDDING

*D*id you know that eight out of ten cats prefer Whiskas? Can you tell Promise spread from butter? Would you exchange one box of Tide for two boxes of any other leading washing powder? Have you tried new Clorox, the bleach that gets you clean round the bend? You have to give it to these advertisers for trying so hard. Over the years they have developed more and more sophisticated techniques of mass persuasion—from those early lithographic posters to the state-of-the-art computer graphics that we have now on TV ads, from old-fashioned sandwich-boards to helium balloons and neon tubes and space-age laser spectaculars. Only the jingles and the slogans remain as fatuous as ever. It can't be easy for those who write them. People are not easily persuaded to buy things, especially in the 1990s.

I suppose in the early days, when advertising was still a novelty, convincing people of the values of a product may have been more straightforward. Certainly one gets the impression from those rather quaint old newspaper commercials for patent medicines that the general public must have been a great deal more gullible in days of old. However, a century of high-pressure advertising has bred a good deal of cynicism in us. We don't take sales talk seriously anymore, or at least we try not to. We are used to the fast patter, the exaggerated claims, the Freudian undertones, and the attention-grabbing gimmickry.

A leading industrialist once said that half the money his company spent on advertising was wasted. "My problem," he said, "is finding out which half!" It takes a very original and a very subtle advertisement these days to really make an impression on the market. Customers in the 1990s are wise to the devices of the hidden persuaders; they aren't easy prey anymore. There is a battle of wits going on out there in the marketplace. The result is, as an exasperated Charlie Brown said in one of the Peanuts cartoons, "You just can't get anybody to believe in you these days."

That atmosphere of public incredulity is not only a problem for would-be salesmen: I am sure that there are a good many political candidates who have encountered a similar entrenched skepticism about their parties' manifestos. Preachers suffer from this kind of consumer resistance too. The suspicion is abroad that the world is full of con men, sharks with a vested interest in making us believe in them.

Advertisers want to make us believe in them so we will buy their product. Politicians want to make us believe in them so we will vote for their party. Preachers want to make us believe in them so that we will join their church. As far as much of the public is concerned, they are all tarred with the same brush. They are all professional propagandists out to manipulate the masses with their eloquence. They aren't really interested in our welfare; they simply want the wealth, or the power, or the prestige that our belief in them will generate. Hence, our sometimes poorly concealed antipathy to such people. "Not today, thank you," we say, as we slam the door in their face. Whether he was hawking encyclopedias or canvassing for the election or had a little booklet in his hand about Jesus, we are just not interested, thank you very much.

It is an understandable reaction; we can't blame people for becoming hostile when they are submitted to this unrelenting torrent of attempted persuasion. The only way to defend ourselves sometimes is to put up the mental barricades.

But there is no denying that it all poses a bit of a problem for the church. How on earth do you communicate the gospel to every creature when the average man or woman in the street today walks around clad in psychological armor plate, embossed with the words "Not today, thank you"? How do you invite faith in Jesus Christ when, as Charlie Brown discovered, you can't get people to believe in anything these days? Of course, some Christians say we should try to compete in the media battle. We should adopt the methods of Madison Avenue ourselves, and market Christianity like toothpaste. They tell us that if we Christians don't make our advertising techniques as sophisticated as the world's, our message won't be heard. There are plenty of examples of that kind of evangelism around today, whether it is the hard sell of the earnest young man, buttonholing strangers with booklets to get them to make a decision, or the soft sell of the charming Christian TV celebrity or singer, projecting an image that is emotionally appealing to modern people and easy to identify with.

I have to say that even when this kind of thing is done in a way that is theologically and morally responsible (and quite often it isn't), I still have doubts about its effectiveness. People are resistant to the gospel today for the same reason as they are resistant to advertising—experience has taught them to be distrustful of sales talk. And much of our evangelism, I'm afraid, sounds like sales talk. How can we bridge that credibility gap? How can we convince the outsider that we really want to share, not to exploit; we really want to give, not take? How can we persuade them to stop treating Christianity like just another of those 57 Heinz-made varieties of religious fanaticism that cranks are peddling around the globe today, and to take the Bible seriously? I believe that in Psalm 34 we have the answer.

A Personal Recommendation

There is one kind of commercial that is as old as humankind itself. It needs no market research, no media hype, no professional expertise, no

Psalm 34

[1]I will extol the LORD at all times;
his praise will always be on my lips.
[2]My soul will boast in the LORD;
let the afflicted hear and rejoice.
[3]Glorify the LORD with me;
let us exalt his name together.

[4]I sought the LORD, and he answered me;
he delivered me from all my fears.
[5]Those who look to him are radiant;
their faces are never covered with
shame.
[6]This poor man called, and the LORD
heard him;
he saved him out of all his troubles.
[7]The angel of the LORD encamps around
those who fear him,
and he delivers them.

[8]Taste and see that the LORD is good;
blessed is the man who takes refuge
in him.
[9]Fear the LORD, you his saints,
for those who fear him lack nothing.
[10]The lions may grow weak and hungry,
but those who seek the LORD lack no
good thing.

[11]Come, my children, listen to me;
I will teach you the fear of the LORD.
[12]Whoever of you loves life
and desires to see many good days,
[13]keep your tongue from evil
and your lips from speaking lies.
[14]Turn from evil and do good;
seek peace and pursue it.

[15]The eyes of the LORD are on the
righteous
and his ears are attentive to their cry;
[16]the face of the LORD is against those
who do evil,
to cut off the memory of them from
the earth.

[17]The righteous cry out, and the LORD
hears them;
he delivers them from all their
troubles.
[18]The LORD is close to the broken-
hearted
and saves those who are crushed in
spirit.

[19]A righteous man may have many
troubles,
but the LORD delivers him from
them all;
[20]he protects all his bones,
not one of them will be broken.

[21]Evil will slay the wicked;
the foes of the righteous will be
condemned.
[22]The LORD redeems his servants;
no one will be condemned who takes
refuge in him.

modern technology, and yet I reckon this type of commercial is still, today, the most effective and compelling, the most irresistible form of persuasion known. I am referring to genuine, personal recommendation.

I stress the word *genuine* because, of course, the advertisers have tried to cash in on personal recommendation as an advertising technique. We don't really believe those housewives who tell us how wonderful their wash has become since they switched to Brand X because we know their lines have been scripted, and we are suspicious that there is a big check waiting for them just off-camera. That sort of contrived testimonial doesn't bridge the credibility gap for us; we write it off just as we write off every other form of advertising. On the other hand, if somebody we know to be honest and we know has no vested interest in the product tells us, on the basis of firsthand experience, that Brand X really is the best thing since sliced bread, we take notice of that. A genuine, personal recommendation carries, even in these days of commercial overkill, an enormous persuasive appeal.

That is exactly what David is offering us here in Psalm 34: "I've been in trouble," he says, "deep trouble. But I have experienced the goodness of God in the most outstanding way in the deliverance I have had from that trouble. And I just long to share that experience with other people who are in trouble too. Taste and see that the Lord is good. I sought the Lord and he answered me. It works; this faith in God business really works; I have proved it. You try it, and see if it doesn't work for you too!" We have a saying: The proof of the pudding is in the eating. "Well," says David, "the same is true of faith in God. The proof of the pudding is in the eating. Taste and see that the Lord is good."

If there is a kind of Christian communication that can breach the psychological defenses of this cynical age that we live in, if there are Christian words that can cross the credibility gap and generate a willingness in people to take the Bible seriously, I am quite convinced this is it: a genuine personal recommendation based on firsthand experience.

> I sought the LORD and he answered me;
>   he delivered me from all my fears.
> Those who look to him are radiant;
>   their faces are never covered with shame.
> This poor man called and the LORD heard him;
>   he saved him out of all his troubles (34:4–6).

101

David speaks here of *fears* and *troubles,* and we find clues that may cast light on what particular fears and troubles he's talking about in the psalm's heading. It locates the writing of this psalm at what was probably one of the most dangerous moments in David's life. We read about it in 1 Samuel 21. David had been forced to flee from the homicidal rage of Saul, the King of Israel. He was penniless, famished, and alone. In his desperation, he sought refuge in the only place he was sure the long arm of Saul couldn't reach him, and that was the land of the Philistines.

Anyone who knows a little of the history of David will know that for David to seek refuge among the Philistines was a bit like a Kuwaiti trying to seek refuge on the streets of Baghdad. The Philistines had a score to settle with David. He was the one who had killed Goliath of Gath, their champion. Indeed, he was the one of whom the young maidens of Israel sang, "Saul has slain his thousands; David has slain his tens of thousands." And it was Philistine thousands they were talking about. David was recognized, captured, and hauled in to appear before the King of Gath. No wonder David speaks in verse 4 of the fears he had. The word used here is a strong word in Hebrew. Brave as he was, David was terrified. There is only one thing to do when you are in such a peril, and that's to pray, which is what David did. He prayed like mad. "I sought the LORD," he says. "This poor man called"—you bet he did!

It must have been as he was praying that he got the idea that we read about in 1 Samuel 21. The King of Gath was a most powerful and dangerous man, but he was not famous for his intelligence. Perhaps, thought David, with God's help, a little piece of play-acting might pull the wool over his eyes. So that is what David tried. Believe it or not, he feigned insanity. He pretended he had gone mad: foaming at the mouth, rolling on the floor, clawing at the furniture with his fingernails, all that sort of stuff.

Sir Laurence Olivier in the role of King Lear couldn't have rendered a more committed performance. And the King of Gath swallowed this little theatrical hook, line, and sinker: "Look at this man," he told his courtiers. "He's insane. Am I so short of lunatics that you have to bring this crazy fool into my court? Get him out of here before he salivates all over the carpet." And to David's great relief, that's

102

what they did; they threw him out, a little manhandled perhaps, but with his head still firmly attached to his body, for which he was profoundly grateful. That, according to Hebrew tradition, was exactly the point in his life when he wrote this song. He composed it on his way out of the court of Gath, on the day he feigned insanity before Abimelech and was driven away a free man.

That's why this psalm is a bit different from the others we have been considering. Those other psalms have, generally speaking, been written in the midst of trouble, as the psalmist is in the very act of wrestling with those negative feelings of depression or guilt or doubt or anxiety; and as a result there has often been a somber gravity about them. Some could even be called laments. This psalm is different. It was composed amid that exuberance you feel when a great weight has suddenly been lifted off your shoulders. This is the sort of psalm you sing the day the exams are over; this is the sort of psalm you sing the day you pass your driving test. David had been scared out of his wits. The King of Gath had only to speak the word and he would have been executed on the spot. But he had gotten away with it. Here he was, David, the great killer of the Philistines, walking scot-free, in broad daylight, in the land of the Philistines.

Incredible! Some of us would call it good luck, but David was shrewd enough to know that there is no such thing. This was not good luck; this was divine deliverance. This was a specific answer to prayer, and he was just thrilled to bits about it.

> I will extol the LORD at all times;
>   his praise will always be on my lips.
> My soul will boast in the LORD;
>   let the afflicted hear and rejoice.
> Glorify the LORD with me;
>   let us exalt his name together (34:1–3).

I can remember when I was a bit younger going on Sunday school bus trips. To pass the time, we would sing different choruses, beginning with each letter of the alphabet in turn. That is what David is doing here although inevitably it gets lost in translation. This psalm is what is called an *acrostic:* each verse begins with one of the twenty-two letters of the Hebrew alphabet, in sequence. Verse 1 begins with the Hebrew letter A; verse 2 begins with the Hebrew letter B; verse 3 begins with letter C, and so on. He must have had fun composing; it is a fun psalm. There is no depression or anxiety about this psalm. David had never felt more positive in his life. Praise just bubbles out of him.

John Bunyan said that the day he was converted, he felt he wanted to tell the crows in the plowed field all about it. He was so full that he couldn't hold it in. That is how David felt that day as he walked out of Gath a free man. He couldn't hold it in: "I am never going to be parsimonious about praising God again," he says. "I am going to praise him morning, noon, and night, irrespective of the circumstances. His praise will at all times be on my lips. For I sought him, and he delivered me from my fears. I called out to him in my helplessness, and he heard me and saved me out of all my troubles. Look at me, folks, I'm radiant! My face is beaming like a halogen-quartz headlamp."

"Believe me," he says, "people who look to God in their troubles always finish up with a glow on their cheeks like that." They are protected; the angel of the Lord surrounds them like the palisade on one of those forts in the old West. The situation may be dire; you may feel terrified, wretched, but God will not let his people be humiliated. At the end of the day, their faces will be flushed, not with embarrassment and shame, but with pride at the great things God has done for them. "My soul will boast in the Lord. Come on, everybody," he says, "let's make it a chorus, not a solo; glorify the Lord with me. Let's exalt his name together!"

This is a salesman's dream. Here's a genuinely satisfied customer—a customer who is not just willing, but anxious, to provide unsolicited and unqualified testimony to God's goodness. Testimony like that merges effortlessly into personal recommendation. Having told us of his own experience, David begins to urge upon us his desire that we should have the experience too.

> Taste and see that the LORD is good;
>> blessed is the man who takes refuge in him.
> Fear the LORD, you his saints,
>> for those who fear him lack nothing.

The lions may grow weak and hungry,
    but those who seek the LORD lack no good thing.

Come, my children, listen to me;
    I will teach you the fear of the LORD (34:8–11).

David almost seems to think it is selfish of him to hoard God's blessing to himself. "I've discovered a wonderful thing," he says. "Faith in God really works. Why don't you try the same experiment I did? I am sure you will get the same results. This isn't Brand X I am talking about, it is the Lord's goodness. You afflicted people of the world, you are in trouble just as I was. Why don't you put the Lord to the test? See if he doesn't meet you at your point of need, just as he met me. Taste and see that the Lord is good. This has my personal recommendation!"

The Price of the Product

It is a compelling challenge coming from the mouth of one with first-hand experience of the Lord's deliverance in his life; he knows what he is talking about. But to give David credit, unlike some salesmen, you'll notice he doesn't neglect to tell you the price. "There are things," he admits, "that you must be ready for, if you are going to sample the Lord's goodness as successfully as I have. In fact, to be precise, there are two things." David then outlines them for us in the following verses.

A Profound Respect for God's Person

I will teach you the fear of the LORD (34:11b).

Notice that phrase *fear of the Lord.* It occurs several times in this psalm. Many of us, perhaps, would have found it more congenial if David had spoken of his love for God, rather than his *fear* of the Lord. But his choice of vocabulary is perhaps not so surprising, bearing in mind that fear had been such a dominant emotion in recent days. In Judea he had been afraid of the jealousy of Saul; in the wilderness he had been afraid of starving to death; in the land of Gath he had been afraid of the cruel vengeance of his captors. One way or another, David had lived on fear for weeks.

105

What then is the answer to fear? According to Rogers and Hammerstein, in *The King and I*, the answer to fear is to whistle a happy tune: "Whenever I feel afraid, I hold my head erect and whistle a happy tune so no one will suspect, I'm afraid." David has something a bit better than deception to recommend. The answer, he says, is not to pretend you aren't afraid. Even if you fool other people, you won't fool yourself. The answer to fear, paradoxically, is to fear. "Fear the LORD, you his saints, for those who fear him lack nothing." A God who isn't big enough to cause you some serious trepidation, is not going to be of much comfort to you when you are trembling on your knees in the court of the Philistines. If he can't make you afraid, he's hardly going to make them afraid. When you are afraid, you need a God on your side who is so tremendous, so dreadful (in the literal meaning of those words), that he is even more formidable than all those things you are in a cold sweat about. As the old paraphrase of this psalm says: "Fear him, you saints, and you will then have nothing else to fear. By comparison all other fears pale into insignificance before the fear of the Lord." One greater than David gave us the very same advice in Luke 12:4–5:

> I tell you, my friends, do not be afraid of those who kill the body and after that can do no more. But I will show you whom you should fear: Fear him who, after the killing of the body, has power to throw you into hell. Yes, I tell you, fear him.

David is telling us in this psalm that if we are going to get to first base in this business of tasting and seeing, then we have to get the fear of God into our hearts. We shall not prove the pudding of God's goodness without a profound and serious respect for God.

A Sincere Commitment to God's Moral Standards

It is said that virtue is its own reward, but David, with a more realistic insight here, is insisting that virtue is rewarded only because God insists that it shall receive a reward. Many people get hold of the wrong end of the stick when it comes to God's commandments. They think of them as the arbitrary rules of a heavenly spoilsport. There is the story of the mother who on hearing an ominous silence from the nursery said to the father, "George, go and find out what the children are doing and make them stop." That is how some people feel God is; he doesn't like us enjoying ourselves. "Find out what they are doing and tell them to stop it"; hence, "Thou shalt not do this, and thou shalt not do that!"

This is quite mistaken; God is no heavenly spoilsport. He doesn't impose the Ten Commandments on us because he wants to spoil our fun. It is simply this: God has designed this world and us to function according to certain moral laws. As the law of gravity constrains us physically, so these laws apply to the moral sphere.

> Whoever of you loves life
>   and desires to see many good days,
> keep your tongue from evil
>   and your lips from speaking lies.
> Turn from evil and do good;
>   seek peace and pursue it (34:12–14).

If people would follow those God-given norms, then human life on this planet would be happy and long. There is no doubt about it. The trouble is, people don't, and that is why life so often is miserable and short.

> The eyes of the LORD are on the righteous
>   and his ears are attentive to their cry;
> the face of the LORD is against those who do evil,
>   to cut off the memory of them from the earth (34:15–16).

This may sound a bit intolerant to liberal, twentieth-century ears; the very idea of God rejecting anybody, turning his back on them, choosing to forget they even existed, is unacceptable to some. But I suspect if you put such a point to David, he would simply reply, "If that's what you think, it is no wonder that your world is in such a mess!" The God who created this universe has moral standards and enforces them, and he intends to go on enforcing them. Complain about that as we will, it is not going to change the situation. We may wave our liberal fists at God all we like and tell him we don't like it; the fact is, he's God and we're not. He will judge us, says the Bible, not by our standards, but by his. There is no way, for all our indignation, that we are ever going to be in the position of judging him, though perhaps we would like to be. No, if we are ever going to taste and see that the Lord is good, you and I have got to get to the point of personal surrender on this matter. He's not asking that we become perfect; but he does insist upon a sincere desire to do things his way. He will not bless rebels.

If we put these two things together: a profound respect for God's person and a sincere commitment to his moral standards, we will have the necessary spiritual foundation for a personal relationship with him. People who have got hold of those two things are the people described as *the righteous* (v. 15) or *his saints* (v. 9). And it is those people David urges to "taste and see that the Lord is good." When such people put God to the test, they prove his goodness.

Perhaps we want to object: "Are you really saying that if I fear God and obey his Word that I am never going to have any more troubles in my life? Are you seriously saying, David, that if I do that, that all my needs will be met, all my problems will be solved, all my anxieties will evaporate away?" We need to pay closer attention to David's words. He is not quite saying that. Indeed, if you think about it, that wasn't even David's own experience. David had troubles, he had fears, but the point he is making here is that when one of God's people is in a tight corner like that, there is something he can do about it that an unbeliever can't. What is that? We have learned it before, and we have to learn it again: he can pray. "His ears are attentive to their cry" (v. 15). "The righteous cry out, and the LORD hears them" (v. 17).

Once again we learn the lesson that the Christian is not immune from trouble. On the contrary, he has many negative experiences. Like David, he is sometimes the victim of other people's jealousy or resentment; like David, he is sometimes hungry, sometimes lonely, sometimes depressed, sometimes afraid. Indeed, like the Master himself, he has a cross to carry. The Bible is quite frank about this. When a Christian finds himself burdened with such troubles, however, he does not have to give way to despair. For his instinct, just like David's, is to cry out and seek the face of the Lord. "This poor man called, and the LORD heard him." That's David's testimony—not a testimony to the absence of troubles, but a testimony to deliverance from troubles in answer to prayer. That is the experience he wants to share with you and me. "Maybe you're sad," he says, "feeling inwardly wounded and bruised. But," he says, "if you are one of God's righteous people, cheer up and pray. 'The LORD is close to the broken hearted and saves those who are crushed in spirit' " (v. 18).

Sometimes we feel weak; we feel that we don't have the strength to cope with the battering life is giving us. David says, "Take courage and pray: 'A righteous man may have many troubles, but the LORD delivers him from them all; he protects all his bones, not one of them will be broken'" (vv. 19–20). Sometimes we feel guilty, tormented by the prospect of God's judgment. "Well," says David, "be reassured and pray: 'Evil will slay the wicked; the foes of the righteous will be condemned. The LORD redeems his servants; no one who takes refuge in him will be condemned' " (vv. 21–22).

It is a promise; all these blessings are there for you to find in a prayer relationship with God, if only you will taste and see his goodness, his loving presence in your sorrow, his strengthening protection in your conflict, his pardoning redemption in your sin and guilt. It is true that the eyes of the Lord are on the righteous and his ears are attentive to their desires. "I know," says David, "because I proved it so. I was at my wits' end, and I took refuge in the Lord. Look at me today, a free man again. This isn't just religious sales talk; this isn't just pious eyewash. I have been through the tunnel of fear and emerged at the other end, praising the Lord. I just wish I could persuade all the other troubled and anxious souls in this world to share my joyful confidence. 'I will extol the LORD at all times. . . . Let the afflicted hear and rejoice.' "

Are You Willing to Testify?

Those of us who are Christians need to ask ourselves: Are we willing, as David so clearly was, to share our personal testimony with others? In days of consumer resistance like ours, this kind of advertisement is the only one that really carries conviction. People need firsthand evidence that Christianity works; they are not going to believe it because a preacher says so. The preacher is just another salesman making a pitch, as far as they are concerned. The success or the failure of the church's evangelistic mission depends not on professional communicators, but on satisfied customers.

In *The Habitation of Dragons*, Keith Miller tells an interesting story in this respect. It is about a man called Joe whom Miller met at one of his meetings when he was preaching one day. Humanly speaking it was a chance encounter, because Joe lived on the other side of the country from Miller, but believe it or not, Joe had arranged to meet his mistress in this town where Miller was preaching. Just as he got out of the car to go to the apartment, three of his friends from home bumped into him on the street. "What are you doing here?" they asked. "Oh, just passing through," lied Joe. "Hey, great, we're just off to hear Keith Miller preach; you must come with us." Afraid to say no lest he gave himself away, Joe went with them. And thus it was that he heard the gospel and that Keith Miller led him to faith in Christ.

About a year later, Miller received a letter from Joe. Joe told him how he had put his faith to work. He'd ended his adulterous relationship, he was trying to live God's way, and things were really so much happier for him as a result. People were beginning to notice. Like David, he really wanted to share the reason for his new-found happiness with his business colleagues, but he was not very accomplished at explaining Christianity. So his purpose in writing was to ask Keith Miller if he would kindly go over to Joe's home town and address this group of people to whom he had testified.

To be honest, it was a very great way to go just to speak to a small company of Joe's friends, but Miller didn't like to discourage his new convert, so he somewhat reluctantly agreed. His plane was late arriving in Joe's town, so he had to be whisked in a car to the hall where the meeting was scheduled to take place. He was more or less taken in through the back door and put straight on the platform. Imagine his surprise, then, when he looked out expecting to see a dozen or so of Joe's business colleagues in front of him, and found instead a hall containing more than eight hundred people, crowded into every corner and aisle. This is what Keith Miller writes about that experience:

> I realized in that moment that all the Christian promotions and programmes; all the evangelistic campaigns, crusades in the world are virtually worthless to motivate people to become Christians, unless they see some ordinary person, like Joe, finding new hope and a new way to live in Christ. Then they will listen.

110

People do not listen to a preacher because his oratory is powerful or his arguments are clever. People listen to a preacher because they see lives transformed in that preacher's congregation. You ask anybody you like, the thing that first attracted them to Jesus Christ was not a sermon; it was a testimony. You and I don't have to win eight hundred pairs of ears, but surely there is somebody, just somebody, out there, who would listen to us when we say to them, "'I sought the Lord, and he answered me.' Why don't you 'taste and see that the Lord is good?'"

Are You Willing to Taste?

But perhaps the thought that is going through somebody's mind as he reads this is, "That is all very well for some, but my problem is that I don't have the kind of firsthand experience of God that would give credibility to that kind of personal recommendation. I don't have a personal prayer relationship with God like David had. I can't say in the personal way he did, 'I sought the Lord and he answered me.'" There are many people like that in the church. David is telling us in this psalm that biblical faith is fundamentally experimental in character: "Taste and see," he says. Many of us want to prove Christianity first and then practice it afterwards. It can't be done. In Christianity by its very nature, proof and practice go hand in hand: the proof of the pudding is in the eating.

Here is a story that illustrates the point. There was an office block in which the whole of one wall of a top-story office was made of glass. The women who had to work in this office did not like it. To their simplistic way of thinking, it seemed that you only had to lean on this fragile pane of glass and down you went. And it was a very long way down. So they went on strike. The management were rather in despair, for you can't change the shape of a building once it has been built. They called in the engineer. He looked at the management. He looked at the window. He looked at the women sitting there, defiant and unconvinced, with their arms folded. Then he had an idea. He walked back the length of the office, ran full tilt at the window, and launched himself at that glass with a shoulder barge that would have looked good on any football field. Then, of course, he bounced back, bruised, but with the window intact.

He was an engineer, you see. He knew the specifications of the glass. He knew that you could drive a truck at that glass and have a hard job breaking it. But though he knew that technically in his mind, it wasn't really an experimental knowledge. Not till his feet were off the ground and his shoulder was against the glass was it experimental. Do you see the difference? We dare not be satisfied with a theoretical knowledge of God; it has to be experimental: "Taste and see."

Not all who want to call themselves Christians are ready for such an experimental engagement with God; they prefer to remain nominal Christians, head-knowledge Christians. They have a secondhand faith only. They have no firsthand personal testimony. I have to be frank and say that such people are very dubious Christians if they are Christians at all. Christianity has to be experimental—"Taste and see." The truth of the Bible has to be experimentally verified, or it hasn't been embraced. The God of the Bible has to be personally known, or he hasn't been encountered.

This is the fundamental difference between reality and formality in religion. There are some people in this world who know God simply as a logical inference; the arguments for the existence of God convince them, so they call themselves Christians. There are some people in this world who know God simply on the basis of hearsay; religion is taken for granted in their social circle, so they call themselves Christians. There are some whose knowledge of God is simply a matter of doctrine; they have studied theology and are persuaded of the orthodoxy of their creed, so they call themselves Christians. But none of these know God as David knew him. The Lord was no philosophical abstraction to him, no social convention to him, no theological formula to him. "I sought the LORD, and he answered me." His was an experimental faith.

We need to ask ourselves whether we can speak in such terms. Is ours a religion of first person pronouns? Or is it just a matter of third person generalizations? Until our knowledge of God embraces that personal dimension, we have not really found the God of the Bible. The proof of the pudding is in the eating. Your partner's faith isn't your faith. Your parents' faith isn't your faith. You must have faith of your own. Agreeing with what the Bible says does not make you a believer. It is true to say, Jesus died for the sins of the world. But believing that doesn't make you a Christian. You become a Christian when you can say from your heart, "He died for me."

7

COUNT YOUR BLESSINGS

According to Shakespeare, one of the cruelest expressions of human selfishness is the failure to say thank you. "Blow, blow, thou winter wind, thou art not so unkind as man's ingratitude." In fact, one of Shakespeare's greatest tragedies, *King Lear*, is really a written illustration of that thought. It is the story of a man who voluntarily abdicates all his noble titles and property in favor of his three daughters, only to find himself reduced to poverty and homelessness as the result of the fact that these daughters cruelly and callously reject him. "Ingratitude, thou marble-hearted fiend," we find King Lear saying. "How sharper than the serpent's tooth it is to have a thankless child."

There are many parents who, while perhaps not quite driven to the pitch of insanity and grief that King Lear was by his daughters, would nevertheless be able to sympathize with his general sentiment. For ungrateful children are, regrettably, an all-too-common feature of modern family life.

I remember, when I lived in Nairobi, hearing the story of a young man called George who was raised in a rural village out in the countryside. George had parents who were not terribly well off, but he was clever and had done well at school and so had secured a place for himself at the university. School is not completely free in Kenya: there are fees to pay, uniforms and books to buy. So getting their son to that high level of educational attainment had placed a great financial demand on his family home. On top of the cash involved there was the additional burden for his aging parents of coping, without his useful energies, on a farm where most sowing and reaping was still done manually. But, needless to say, his parents felt no resentment at their sacrifice. They were full of pride on the day they heard that their son was to graduate from the university. Their best clothes were ill-fitting and old-fashioned by our standards, but they put them on, caught the rickety old bus up to the capital city to see their son gain his diploma. They could think of no honor more wonderful than to stand beside him in his academic gown and be introduced as George's parents.

Yet George had changed in his days in the capital city. When he recognized his parents in the assembling crowds on the university campus, and saw how shabby they looked in comparison with the rich friends he had acquired for himself at college, he ignored them out of embarrassment. He walked away; he ignored them as if he didn't know them. I doubt whether his father had ever heard of *King Lear*, let alone read it, but he certainly knew that day what the Bard meant when he said, "How sharper than a serpent's tooth it is to have a thankless child."

I suppose some might be tempted to say that George's parents must have asked for the treatment they got. Obviously, they had overindulged the boy; they had given him too much, too easily, and turned him into a spoiled brat. For all I know perhaps they had. But it would be unfair to overgeneralize on that score. As a pastor, one has all too often heard the sighs and tears of parents complaining desperately, "Where did we go wrong?" And the fact is that you cannot always find an answer to that question. Sometimes the best and most balanced of homes seems to produce ungrateful wretches. It will not do to assume that it has to be the parents' fault. The fact is that we human beings are not robots, mindlessly playing out the programming of our childhood conditioning. We are responsible individuals. George, spoiled brat or not, had a choice to

---

Psalm 103

[1]Praise the LORD, O my soul;
  all my inmost being, praise his holy
  name.
[2]Praise the LORD, O my soul,
  and forget not all his benefits—
[3]who forgives all your sins
  and heals all your diseases,
[4]who redeems your life from the pit
  and crowns you with love
  and compassion,
[5]who satisfies your desires with good
  things
  so that your youth is renewed like the
  eagle's.

[6]The LORD works righteousness
  and justice for all the oppressed.

[7]He made known his ways to Moses,
  his deeds to the people of Israel:
[8]The LORD is compassionate and gracious,
  slow to anger, abounding in love.
[9]He will not always accuse,
  nor will he harbor his anger forever;
[10]he does not treat us as our sins deserve
  or repay us according to our iniquities.
[11]For as high as the heavens are above the
  earth,
  so great is his love for those who fear
  him;
[12]as far as the east is from the west,

so far has he removed our transgressions from us.
[13]As a father has compassion on his
  children,
  so the LORD has compassion on those
  who fear him;
[14]for he knows how we are formed,
  he remembers that we are dust.
[15]As for man, his days are like grass,
  he flourishes like a flower of the field;
[16]the wind blows over it and it is gone,
  and its place remembers it no more.
[17]But from everlasting to everlasting
  the LORD's love is with those who
  fear him,
  and his righteousness with their children's children—
[18]with those who keep his covenant
  and remember to obey his precepts.

[19]The LORD has established his throne
  in heaven,
  and his kingdom rules over all.

[20]Praise the LORD, you his angels,
  you mighty ones who do his bidding,
  who obey his word.
[21]Praise the LORD, all his heavenly hosts,
  you his servants who do his will.
[22]Praise the LORD, all his works
  everywhere in his dominion.

Praise the LORD, O my soul.

---

make that day: he had the power either to display gratitude or ingratitude to his parents. The same choice is ours as we read Psalm 103.

Notice how the psalm begins and in fact how it also ends: "Praise the LORD, O my soul." David here is not talking, as he usually does in the psalms, to God; he is talking to himself. To his *soul,* as he puts it. In fact, he continues that conversation with himself all through the first five verses. He is telling himself the things he feels he needs to hear. He had enough insight into his own perversity to recognize how easily he could slide, like George, into being a thankless child. David knew how little God deserves such cruel treatment, so he determined to make sure that there was at least one song in his repertoire to act as a deterrent to any such ungrateful attitude: a song that is not so much a psalm of praise in itself, as an exhortation to praise. There is an old hymn in our hymnbook that espouses the same purpose: "Count Your Blessings." It lacks the poetic genius of David's psalm, and the tune it is set to doesn't have too much musical merit either, in my judgment, but it is at least trying to do the same kind of thing that David is in Psalm 103. He is cataloging the goodness of God; he is enumerating his blessings, lest in a moment of depression or backsliding, he should forget the source of his prosperity and take God's grace for granted.

That is an exhortation we all need to hear. If you have any doubt that sometimes good parents suffer the pain of thankless children, then just think about the way in which the world treats God. He is a Father who has been good to us in a thousand and one ways: never overindulgent, disciplining us when we need it by negative experiences, and certainly never giving us everything we want the moment we want it. And yet his kindness to us is vast, showering blessings upon us daily. Today, however, the vast majority of men and women turn their backs on God, just as surely as George turned his back on his parents on that university campus. They ignore his goodness. In their selfishness and complacency they take it all for granted. Not one word of thanks is offered to him.

Psalm 103 is a preventive against that kind of ingratitude. "Count your blessings," David advises himself; and in doing so, he advises us too. As we study the psalm we will endeavor to answer three questions that will encourage us in the business of counting our blessings.

Why Was David So Sure
That He Had Blessings to Count?

Our Personal Experience

> who forgives all your sins
>   and heals all your diseases,
> who redeems your life from the pit
>   and crowns you with love and compassion,
> who satisfies your desires with good things
>   so that your youth is renewed like the eagle's (103:3–5).

The first reason David was sure he had blessings from God to celebrate was rooted in his own personal experience. It is quite clear from these verses that David composed this psalm in the wake of some fairly recent deliverance. The close link between sin and disease in verse 3 suggests that it was associated with an incident in David's life when he had seriously grieved God and been chastened with some kind of physical infirmity as a result. There are a number of incidents in David's life that might correspond to that. It isn't true, of course, that all illness is the direct result of personal sin. That wasn't true for Job; neither was it true of a blind man that Jesus met. When the disciples asked him, "Who sinned, this man or his parents, that he was born blind?" Jesus very significantly replied "Neither." In this fallen world the pain isn't parcelled out in direct proportion to people's guilt; sometimes the innocent suffer. The Bible recognizes that very candidly; in fact, there is a cross set at the very heart of the Bible's message that declares that message more plainly than anything.

It must also be said, however, that sometimes disease and sin are linked in human experience. In fact, we all know that is true. The anxiety associated with guilt can produce ulcers. The infections associated with sexual misbehavior can produce AIDS. We don't know the details of David's recent illness, but clearly he felt that he had brought it on himself by his moral failure. What's more it had been a serious, life-threatening condition. David had, for a while, felt himself hovering on the edge of death, or "the pit" as he rather graphically refers to it in verse 4. Yet now this personal crisis has passed; David is sure that the sin that had given rise to the situation had been resolved, the ill-

117

ness cured, the death sentence remitted. Indeed, it seems from verse 5 that David was now feeling fitter than for many years: "my youth is renewed like the eagle's."

To what then does David attribute this remarkable recovery? Does he attribute it to the medical care given to him by the court physician? Or to the good fortune promised to him in his astrologer's horoscope? No, David is a believer, and because he is, he sees this deliverance as nothing less than a demonstration of God's personal involvement in his life. "He forgives all my sins; he heals all my diseases. He redeems my life from the pit; he crowns me, king though I am, with a coronation no doctor can provide. He crowns me with love and compassion."

Now of course the skeptic may want to ask why David felt so secure in explaining the deliverance he had experienced in this way. After all, if God really cared for David, why did he let him get ill in the first place? If God really cared for David, why did he allow him to get so terrifyingly close to death? If you say it is all because of the sin in his life, then what about all those good people who don't recover from their illnesses; and what about all those bad people who never get sick in the first place?

David's moral interpretation of his poor health here, and his theological interpretation of his restoration to fitness is, to say the very least, arbitrary. There must be a dozen alternative explanations of his experience that fit the facts just as well. How can he be so sure that he is right to attribute his deliverance to God's blessing in his life?

David is not without an answer to that challenge.

God's Revelation of Himself

> The LORD works righteousness
> and justice for all the oppressed.
>
> He made known his ways to Moses,
> his deeds to the people of Israel (103:6–7).

Notice that David has moved on from addressing his soul subjectively, and is now making more comprehensive objective statements about God's dealings with his people generally, in Bible history. "My personal experience in this matter," says David, "is an illustration of a general truth about God that I find taught in the Scriptures." In the days of Moses, God broke through into the experience, not just of an isolated individual, but of an entire nation. He demonstrated then the kind of just and righteous God he is by delivering them from oppression in Egypt; he demonstrated the kind of consistent God he is by punishing them when they disobeyed him in the wilderness; and he demonstrated the kind of faithful God he is by persevering with them in spite of all their failures and seeing them into the Land of Canaan, just as he promised them.

In all his dealings with his people during this cardinal period of self-disclosure, God showed himself to be "compassionate and gracious, slow to anger, abounding in love" (v. 8).

This isn't just David's own verdict on the history of Israel. He is actually quoting from Exodus 34:6, the very words God himself had spoken to Moses after the children of Israel had lapsed into the idolatrous worship of the golden calf. The Lord then appeared to Moses in a cloud, proclaiming, "The LORD, the LORD, the compassionate and gracious God, slow to anger, abounding in love and faithfulness, maintaining love to thousands, and forgiving wickedness, rebellion and sin." We are told that on that occasion Moses fell to the ground and worshiped God: "'O Lord, if I have found favor in your eyes,' he said, 'then let the Lord go with us. Although this is a stiff-necked people, forgive our wickedness and our sin, and take us as your inheritance'" (Exod. 34:9).

David, by quoting that passage, is drawing a direct line between the experience of the people of Israel in the Book of Exodus and his own personal experience. His interpretation of his healing as a demonstration of God's blessing is not some fantasy, dreamed up while he was feeling feverish. No, he is recognizing the same pattern of divine providence, judgment, and grace as God's people down through the ages have constantly witnessed. Just as the Israelites found mercy in their idolatry, so David had found mercy in his sin. Just as they were delivered from Egypt, so he was delivered from sickness. He's making a connection between what the Bible told him and what in his own life he had experienced.

Now this, of course, is how it is for every believer. We can't prove God is at work in our lives, not scientifically. We can't prove that he answers our prayers. If the skeptic wants to interpret events in some other way, we can't prove him wrong. All we can say is that our per-

119

sonal experience and the testimony of the Bible mesh together in such a way that we find it utterly, personally convincing. We know God is real because somehow the whole thing hangs together and fits. It rings true.

That insight may be a help to somebody looking for faith. I know when I first started exploring Christianity many years ago, I wanted some kind of logical argument that ended, God exists. Q.E.D. There you are; it's proven! I felt cheated when I discovered that the Bible never even tried to offer me any such chain of reasoning. Then I realized that faith, as the Bible understands it, isn't a logical deduction. You don't prove God exists and then decide you are going to believe in him because you have proved it. As an ancient father of the church said, "I have to believe in order to understand." Faith isn't a logical deduction; it is much closer to what scientists sometimes call these days a "paradigm shift."

In the Middle Ages everybody believed that the earth was the center of the universe. That was all right as far as it went; it could explain the motion of the stars and the sun. Unfortunately, there were the planets—they wouldn't behave themselves! They went all over the place; you just couldn't explain their behavior at all. That's why they're called *planets*—literally "wandering ones." Then along came Copernicus and Galileo. They had this extraordinary intuition: maybe the sun is the center, not the earth. They couldn't prove it, but they simply discovered that if you looked at things that way, it all fit in a much more satisfying fashion. The planets' movement made sense, then. There was no line of logical reasoning that ended Q.E.D., but once they had made the mental leap to see things in this new heliocentric way, they just knew it had to be true. It fit. It rang true. In the same way, when faith comes to us, it never comes with a feeling of self-congratulation: "At last I've proved it!" It comes with a sense of revelation: "At last, I see it now!" Faith is a new way of looking at the world that makes much more convincing sense of it.

David wasn't speculating, then, when he spoke of a God who forgives his sin and heals his diseases. He was discovering what believing men and women in every age have discovered: that the Bible makes compelling sense of human experience. As C. S. Lewis once put it: "I believe in God for the same reason I believe in the sun; not because I can see it, but because I see everything else by it." That is why David was so sure. God had proven himself in his experience to be the same God he had declared himself to be in the Bible. The Bible and his experience meshed together. If you come to faith, that's how it will feel for you.

What Particular Blessings Was David Anxious to Enumerate?

The answer to this question is found in verses 9–14. We can sum it up in a single word: grace.

David could have listed all kinds of blessings here when he says, "Praise the LORD, O my soul, and forget not all his benefits": blessings of daily food, of political peace and prosperity in the land, of safety in journeying, of physical health. But that isn't where he puts his focus. This whole catalogue of blessings that we find listed in verses 9–14 is really just a development of the truth about God that Moses had affirmed in that text from Exodus, and that David's own experience had confirmed in his recent deliverance: that God is a God of grace, pardoning grace.

The Reluctance of God's Anger

> He will not always accuse,
> nor will he harbor his anger forever (103:9).

"There is something about God's very nature," says David, "that dislikes staying angry." Undoubtedly, his wrath is real; David knew that. But as Martin Luther once put it, "Wrath is God's strange work." Anger is an alien attribute for God. It is called into existence by something external to God's own person, namely sin. It isn't an eternal attribute in God's personality in the same way that love is. There was a time before the world was made when there was no anger at all in the heart of God, for there was no sin to provoke it. The Bible tells us equally that there will be a time in the future when, in the new heavens and new earth, there will be nothing to rouse God's anger. For all things in heaven and earth will be reconciled to him.

121

The Generosity of God's Mercy

> he does not treat us as our sins deserve
>   or repay us according to our iniquities (103:10).

There was an incident in the life of Napoleon when he ordered a young deserter who was brought before him to be shot. Whereupon the young man's mother came forward and begged for her son's life: "Have mercy on him," she pleaded with Napoleon. Napoleon imperiously retorted, "He doesn't deserve any mercy." Whereupon the woman replied, "If he deserved it, it would not be mercy." It is a good point, isn't it? In days like ours, where capitalism dominates the economics of our society, I suspect that many people find it hard to value, or even understand, mercy. If you deserve it, you should get it; if you don't deserve it, you shouldn't get it. That's the philosophy of the marketplace. Thank goodness it is not the philosophy of heaven. God does not treat us as our sins deserve; he does not repay us according to our iniquities. If he did, there would be no hope for us.

The Magnitude of God's Love

> For as high as the heavens are above the earth,
>   so great is his love for those who fear him (103:11).

You must have seen a child sometimes playing that game with its parents: "How much do you love me?" The arms are widened; "This much? This much? No, this much." When David plays that game with God, his arms simply aren't long enough. When it comes to demonstrating how much God loves him, the universe itself could scarcely have contained the ruler that was necessary to measure the vast dimensions involved.

The Comprehensiveness of God's Forgiveness

> as far as the east is from the west,
>   so far has he removed our transgressions from us (103:12).

I suppose some might say that with the advent of intercontinental air flight, David's illustration has lost some of its force. Traveling by air, one is always amazed to discover how little time elapses between

122

leaving the sun setting in the west and rediscovering it dawning again in the east. But perhaps the idea of distance isn't actually what's in David's mind here. Maybe the thing that he's trying to point out to us is that however many miles you think lie between west and east, you cannot look two ways at once. You can't witness the sunset and the sunrise simultaneously. You have to turn your back on one in order to see the other. So, he is saying, when God forgives us, he puts our sins and us on two different horizons. So when he looks at our sin, he is no longer looking at us, and when he looks at us, he is no longer looking at our sin. To use the vocabulary of Paul, he has justified us. He has found a way of detaching our sin from us, so that he can condemn the one, without condemning the other. In that sense, twentieth century or not, David's metaphor is still matchless.

The Tenderness of God's Compassion

> As a father has compassion on his children,
>   so the LORD has compassion on those who fear him (103:13).

I can never read those lines without recalling that most exquisite of all Jesus' parables. I see that prodigal son, drooping homeward, his shoulders bowed with shame and humiliation, his knees trembling with guilty fear, wondering how on earth his father is going to receive him when he has wounded him so. Talk about filial ingratitude, George had nothing on the prodigal. Here was a son who had told his father, "I wish you were dead! I like the money bequeathed in your will better than I like you, Dad! Why make me wait for the funeral? I want it now." And yet there he was, returning home, a failure driven by hunger and remorse to the father he had so cruelly and ungratefully spurned. And what does Jesus say? "When his father saw him, while he was still a great way off, he was filled with compassion for him." Make no mistake about it, the God of the Bible *feels*. Those unruly and problematic emotions of ours are an echo, within the divine image that we human beings bear, of passions that tear the very heart of God.

The Intimacy of God's Understanding

> for he knows how we are formed,
>   he remembers that we are dust (103:14).

123

To know all may not be to forgive all, but it may very well be to forgive a great deal. The Lord knows everything there is to know about us. There is not a molecule he didn't personally design. He understands the complexity of our brains; he understands the unpredictability of our feelings; he understands the subtleties of our genetics; he understands the powerful influence of our conditioning; he understands the lusts of our flesh and the temptations of Satan; he understands the mystery of birth and the terror of death. He understands all these things; there is absolutely nothing about a human being that God does not know. That being so, he knows far better than to overestimate us. What was it Jesus said in the Garden of Gethsemane to his disciples? "The spirit is willing but the flesh is weak." Too true, it is. Jesus knew better than to engage in any utopian optimism about the essential goodness of the human race. He knew Judas would betray him; he knew Peter would deny him. He knows that's how human beings are. And he is realistic enough to make allowances for such frailty.

The Dependability of God's Faithfulness

> As for man, his days are like grass,
>   he flourishes like a flower of the field;
> the wind blows over it and it is gone,
>   and its place remembers it no more.
> But from everlasting to everlasting
>   the LORD's love is with those who fear him,
>   and his righteousness with their children's children—
> with those who keep his covenant
>   and remember to obey his precepts (103:15–18).

There was a time when as a child, I thought the prospect of living to be seventy was an eternity. I'm now over halfway, and I have discovered that eternity has grown marvelously short! It is not till we get to our adult years that we realize how painfully ephemeral human life really is. You and I will die, sooner perhaps than we expect; sooner, probably, than we want. One can only pity this shallow culture of ours that must try to hide the truth of our mortality behind conspiracies of silence. David is right: "As for man, his days are like grass." Our loved ones may treasure our memory, but they will die too eventually. Even if we have been notable authors, our books will go out of print. Even the very name on our gravestone will be rendered indecipherable eventually by the ravages of the wind and the weather. "He flourishes like a flower of the field; the wind blows over it and it is gone, and its place remembers it no more." It is an unpalatable truth that David speaks. How then are we to escape the appalling meaninglessness of it all? Cyril Connolly once wrote, "The emptiness of life is more dreadful than its misery."

There is only one refuge from the sense of futility that inevitably descends like a chill wind on our hearts when we think too long about our own destiny, and that is to find an eternal home in the heart of God. The world may forget us, but God never will. The weather may erase our names from the gravestone, but it will not erase our names from his heart. "From everlasting to everlasting," says David, "the LORD's love is with those who fear him" (103:17). Those skilled in Hebrew will point out that David's language here may mean no more than that God will be faithful to his people *as a whole,* from age to age. But remember this is the same man who wrote ". . . you will not abandon me to the grave, . . . you have made known to me the path of life; you will fill me with joy in your presence, with eternal pleasures at your right hand" (Ps. 16:10–11). This is the man who wrote: "Goodness and mercy will follow me all the days of my life, and I will dwell in the house of the LORD forever" (Ps. 23:6). For that reason I don't think it is illegitimate to suggest that David's assurance of God's eternal faithfulness here extends to him as an individual, as well as to his posterity. So secure is this relationship David has with God that he cannot imagine anything, even death, severing it. A God who loves him enough to pardon his sins, a God who loves him enough to call him his child, such a God surely loves him enough to want their friendship to survive beyond the grave.

God's Control over the Universe

> The LORD has established his throne in heaven,
> and his kingdom rules over all (103:19).

You want blessings—then David has plenty. His God is a God of reluctant anger and generous mercy, of immeasurable love and radical forgiveness; a God of paternal tenderness and sympathetic understanding; a God of unchanging character and everlasting grace. David brings his octave of eulogy to a conclusion by celebrating the God who is in sole control of the universe. He is thwarted by no unforeseen circumstances; he is usurped by no hostile powers. This God possesses unchallenged supremacy in heaven and earth. This God must win.

What Response Did David Feel He Owed to a God of Such Blessings?

> Praise the LORD, you his angels,
>   you mighty ones who do his bidding,
>   who obey his word.
> Praise the LORD, all his heavenly hosts,
>   you his servants who do his will.
> Praise the LORD, all his works
>   everywhere in his dominion (103:20–22a).

And within the context of that universal praise, David sets his own:

> Praise the LORD, O my soul (103:22b).

We need to ask ourselves whether or not there is any real praise in our hearts. It is so easy to come to church out of habit. It is so easy to recite hymns mindlessly. It is so easy to repeat *Amen* without ever really speaking to God. It is so easy to hear sermons without ever really listening to God. Spiritual lukewarmness is a common disease in a land like ours where being a Christian is respectable. If that is our condition then we, like David, need to talk to ourselves. We need to stir our hearts up to a more appropriate emotional response to the truth about the God we know. If you find your heart cold, then do what David did and count your blessings.

It is hard to believe that anybody could be more blessed than David was; but I assure you, if you are a Christian then you are. For David, great saint that he was, knew little or nothing of the spiritual blessings that are ours in Christ Jesus. When he tried to find a measure for God's love, the best he could do was to look at the height of the sky. You and I can do better. There is a cross on that hillside called Calvary, which for us is a far greater measure of the love of God than even the unfathomable depths of the universe. The arms of the cross fling wide to show us the passion that tears the heart of God because of our sin. You are right, David, God does not treat us as our sins deserve. He has not just removed our transgressions from us to infinite distance; he has placed those sins on himself and borne the penalty for them. You think you are blessed, David, because God has redeemed your life from the pit of death? He has redeemed our souls from the pit of hell! We have blessings to count, David, that you have not even dreamt of.

That being so, should we not find it in our hearts to praise God? Should it not be a joy and a delight to us to praise God? We must not be satisfied with a perfunctory nod in God's direction on Sunday morning. We must shake off that apathy, fight down that depression, repent of that rebelliousness. We need to instruct our souls to give God the praise that is due to his name.

Those who do not consider themselves yet to be Christians have a question to ask themselves too: Do you have any blessings from God to count? I ask that question seriously in case some are misled. It may have seemed that these divine blessings that David is enumerating here belong to everybody. If you look carefully at what David says, you will see that he says it is not so.

> But from everlasting to everlasting
>> the LORD's love is with those who fear him,
>> and his righteousness with their children's children—
> with those who keep his covenant
>> and remember to obey his precepts (103:17–18).

David could have written about God's common blessings to all humanity, but he did not. Instead, in this psalm he is counting the special blessings that belong to God's own people. The experience of pardoning grace is not universal, and because this is so, it is not just ungrateful to take it for granted, but it can be dangerous. Has God removed your transgressions as far as the east is from the west? Has he pledged his fatherly compassion to you? Have you got any blessings that count? Any real, spiritual, eternal blessings?

127

You can have. These blessings can be yours, and you need to make sure they are yours. They are the privilege of those who have a covenant relationship with God, a relationship such as David knew. The Bible's message is that we can have such a relationship. When we come back to God as that erring prodigal came back in the story; when we pledge to him a new obedience, a new respect, a new commitment; when such a relationship begins, then God's pardoning grace becomes ours. We can start counting our blessings too—and gratefully.

8

DELIVERANCE FROM CRISIS

One moment they were dancing to the music of the disco and the next they found themselves in the tidal waters of the Thames. Said one young female survivor: "I just prayed to God." It is interesting how often when we are in a situation like that, where our life hangs in the balance, that we pray to God. Often, of course, it is no more than an involuntary cry of terror or a superstitious clutching at straws. But not always. Sometimes such prayers are the watershed of a real, spiritual change in a person's life.

It is at moments like that, moments of real panic when we know our lives may be shortly coming to an end, that the ultimate questions of our existence are forced upon us. It is a moment of truth. The urgency of the situation demands that we can no longer prevaricate or pretend about spiritual things; we have to make up our minds, once and for all. We have to decide for God or against him.

I remember my father-in-law telling me how he had arrived at such a critical moment in his life on the deck of a torpedoed merchant ship during the last war. As the rebellious son of rather strict Christian parents, he had gone to sea to escape the confining discipline of his family. He told me that as he prepared himself to jump into the ocean

---

Psalm 116

¹I love the LORD, for he heard my voice;
 he heard my cry for mercy.
²Because he turned his ear to me,
 I will call on him as long as I live.

³The cords of death entangled me,
 the anguish of the grave came upon
 me;
 I was overcome by trouble and
 sorrow.
⁴Then I called on the name of the LORD:
 "O LORD, save me!"

⁵The LORD is gracious and righteous;
 our God is full of compassion.
⁶The LORD protects the simplehearted;
 when I was in great need, he saved me.

⁷Be at rest once more, O my soul,
 for the LORD has been good to you.

⁸For you, O LORD, have delivered my
 soul from death,
 my eyes from tears,
 my feet from stumbling,
⁹that I may walk before the LORD
 in the land of the living.

¹⁰I believed; therefore I said,
 "I am greatly afflicted."
¹¹And in my dismay I said,
 "All men are liars."

¹²How can I repay the LORD
 for all his goodness to me?
¹³I will lift up the cup of salvation
 and call on the name of the LORD.
¹⁴I will fulfill my vows to the LORD
 in the presence of all his people.

¹⁵Precious in the sight of the LORD
 is the death of his saints.
¹⁶O LORD, truly I am your servant;
 I am your servant, the son of your
 maidservant;
 you have freed me from my chains.

¹⁷I will sacrifice a thank offering to you
 and call on the name of the LORD.
¹⁸I will fulfill my vows to the LORD
 in the presence of all his people,
¹⁹in the courts of the house of the
 LORD—
 in your midst, O Jerusalem.

Praise the LORD.

---

from that sinking ship, he felt rather like Jonah. He discovered that running away from God was less easy than running away from home.

Psalm 116 is quite clearly born out of a similar experience. It was written in the aftermath of a crisis. The emergency had passed, so like Psalm 103 it is a hymn of thanksgiving, expressing the psalmist's gratitude to God for his deliverance. But in this psalm the memory of what he had been through is much more vivid and recent. As a result, it is charged with much more emotional intensity and is expressed in a much more personal way. The pronouns *I* and *me* and *my* dominate almost every verse.

Try to identify with the psalmist's experience. Try to get into his shoes. Try to feel with him the panic of this crisis period of his life, and the excitement of the spiritual discovery that accompanied it.

A Dangerous Situation

> The cords of death entangled me,
>> the anguish of the grave came upon me;
>> I was overcome by trouble and sorrow (116:3).

The psalmist is using language here borrowed from Psalm 18, when David was going through a particularly dangerous period of his political career. That metaphor, "The cords of the grave are coiled around me," has almost a nightmarish quality from a horror movie: "I felt the icy fingers of death reaching out from the grave and clutching at me." What the precise nature of this mortal peril was, he doesn't tell us. We can only speculate that it was a serious illness. But it is equally possible that, just as in David's case in Psalm 18, the threat to his life was from a human agency. Either way it was clearly a dangerous situation, and it reduced the psalmist to a state of total emotional collapse. "I was overcome by trouble and sorrow," he says.

I guess not many of us have actually had to face the prospect of death in this very direct way. Perhaps the closest that some of us have come was that near miss when we were driving on the freeway; we swerved and in that moment our hearts were in our mouths. Fortunately, that sort of panic only lasts a second or two, so such experiences don't really devastate us. A raised pulse, a temporary tremor in the hand, is all that it leaves us with. But to really understand what the psalmist is talking about here, you must imagine living with that level of anxiety that perhaps you felt for a few brief seconds, week after week, month after month.

Soldiers who came back from the First World War suffering from combat fatigue knew all about it; so do victims of torture and brainwashing. Psychiatrists map such experiences quite accurately now. They know that such sustained stress slowly but surely pulverizes the nervous system of even the strongest men and women. Perhaps it is among the victims of such mental breakdown that we are most likely to find those people who are in the best position to empathize with this sense of melancholy hopelessness to which the psalmist is driven. Notice that phrase again in verse 3: "the anguish of the grave came upon me." The Hebrew suggests a feeling of being dragged into terrifying darkness. One commentator expresses it very vividly when he writes: "The walls of hell closed in on me." This psalmist was scared, almost literally, clean out of his wits.

A Desperate Prayer

> Then I called on the name of the LORD:
> "O LORD, save me!" (116:4).

Notice the reaction this dangerous situation generated. It gave rise to anxiety and terror, but also, to prayer—a desperate prayer, first of all. He uses quite a rare Hebrew interjection that adds great emphasis to his plea. I have no doubt this man had prayed before; but never with such passion, never with such urgency, and never, I suspect, with such persistence. The imperfect tense could, perhaps, be rendered "kept on calling and calling." This moment of crisis had stripped him of all his usual self-confidence. Not only did he feel completely unable to help himself, but there was nobody else around who was able to comfort and assist him either. On the contrary, those people he thought he could depend upon had proven utterly unreliable.

See how he speaks of them in verse 11: "And in my dismay I said, 'All men are liars.'" That might imply, I suppose, that the source of this threat to his life was treacherous individuals who were murderously conspiring against him. Or it could simply be that in his trouble, he had sought help from his friends, and they had proved to be broken reeds who had deserted him in his hour of need. Either way, it is clear that the psalmist was feeling bitterly disillusioned with people. The perfidiousness of the human race just exacerbated his feelings of vulnerability. He speaks of *dismay,* a word that has connotations of trepidation, and even panic. For if there is one thing worse than feeling afraid, it is feeling afraid *alone.* And alone is how he felt.

Yet, in the midst of his isolation and insecurity, he discovered something about himself that seems almost to have taken him by surprise. He tells us about it in verse 10: "I believed," he says. Unfortunately, the precise meaning of the verse is not absolutely clear. The Hebrew conjunction that is translated "therefore" can be taken several ways. You could, for instance, render the verse as the NIV margin does, "I believed *even when* I said I was greatly afflicted," though that seems to strike a rather smug note which does not fit easily with the mood of total helplessness the psalmist is confessing. It is as if he was rather congratulating himself on how tenacious his faith had really been in spite of all his pessimistic comments.

Another version renders it: "I believed *even though* I said I am greatly afflicted." That, at least, has a more apologetic tone, as if the writer is saying, "Well, my faith survived though I have to admit it was in pretty poor shape, as evidenced by all my whining and self-pitying complaints."

You could even translate it: "I believed *because* I said I am greatly afflicted." Rendered that way, the psalmist is implying that faith was for him a leap of despair in a situation in which he felt he had no other course of action: "I believed because I was at my wits' end and there was no alternative."

But I have to say I have a suspicion that the NIV translation is right to render the text as it does, "I believed; *therefore* I said, 'I am greatly afflicted.'" In many ways, that is the most natural rendering of the Hebrew, and it is certainly closest to the way the apostle Paul, in 2 Corinthians, and the Septuagint Greek translation of the Old Testament understood this verse. Taken that way, the statements that follow— "I am greatly afflicted" and "All men are liars"—cease to be sullen and peevish soliloquies and become, instead, piercing insights into the content of the prayer that the psalmist prayed in his desperation.

133

He is saying: "In my moment of crisis, I discovered I was a believer, a real believer, not just a nominal churchgoer, and the faith that I discovered enabled me to verbalize my distraught emotions, not just to myself, but to God. I told him exactly how I felt; I told him how miserable I was in the situation I was in. 'I am greatly afflicted,' I told him. I told him how hurt I had been by the treachery of my friends. 'All men are liars,' I said to him. I didn't put on any mask of pious triumphalism, I didn't have to. In the extremity of my helplessness and hopelessness I discovered a relationship of trust with God that liberated me from all pretentiousness. In that situation, there was only one thing I could be with this God, and that is honest, brutally honest. Maybe that's why he listened, for listen he did. I tell you I never realized it was possible to feel so much devotion for God, until the day I realized he paid attention to me, deliberately turning his ear to my prayer. I love the Lord, for he heard my voice."

A Divine Initiative

> The LORD is gracious and righteous;
>   our God is full of compassion.
> The LORD protects the simplehearted;
>   when I was in great need, he saved me (116:5–6).

It isn't hard to feel the wave of relief and gratitude that sweeps over our poet just in the recollection of this narrow escape. That peril to his life, whatever it was, had gone, and just like David in Psalm 103, spiritual intuition convinces him that it is not just a lucky break. This is not just coincidence; this is an answer to prayer. God had stepped into his life and answered his desperate plea. It must have been a quite recent event because judging from verse 7, his emotions had still not fully recovered.

> Be at rest once more, O my soul,
>   for the LORD has been good to you.

That is very true to life. There is a kind of inertia in our psychological makeup that you often observe in people who have gone through a traumatic experience. It takes time to restore the emotional equilibrium. Just as a fireman might reassure a terrified child he has just rescued from the burning building, so the psalmist here has to counsel his own racing heart: "It's OK, relax. It's all over, you're safe now. Be at rest once more, O my soul."

But even allowing for that, it is quite clear that the psalmist is already an altogether more composed person than he had once been.

> For you, O LORD, have delivered my soul from death,
>   my eyes from tears,
>   my feet from stumbling (116:8).

I find something particularly touching about that line "my eyes from tears." He is quoting from another psalm of David here, Psalm 56:13. But there David had only written, "You have delivered my soul from death and my feet from stumbling." That additional line, "my eyes from tears," is our poet's personal insertion, his own composition. And it surely indicates just how emotionally broken he had been by his ordeal. Tears had been a major part of his life in recent months. Perhaps it is not too much to say this devastating experience had reduced him to a blubbering heap. But not any longer. No, the Lord had delivered him. How precisely he had done it, he doesn't detail for us. What he does share with us are the conclusions he had arrived at as to why God had intervened in his life in this saving way.

God Pitied His Simplicity

> The LORD protects the simplehearted (116:6).

Gracious, righteous, compassionate God that he is, he protects the simplehearted; and when such people are in great need, he saves them. That phrase *simplehearted* might sound as if this divine intervention was a reward for the psalmist's virtue of humility, but that would be to misunderstand the text. In fact, a better translation would be, not the "simplehearted," but the "simpleminded." Almost always in the Old Testament this Hebrew word is used in a pejorative sense; it describes someone who is inexperienced and gullible—simple, in the worst sense of that word.

The simplehearted person is the dupe who will believe anything he is told. Indeed, by using this word here, the psalmist may be suggest-

135

ing that he feels he got himself into this mess he's been talking about. He had stupidly trusted people that a wiser man would have held in suspicion. If that is how it was, God certainly didn't chasten him for his folly. There is no serves-you-right attitude. No, on the contrary, the psalmist found in God a stalwart ally against the ruthless and cunning sharks who thought to exploit the naivete of a greenhorn like him.

God Valued His Life

> Precious in the sight of the LORD
>   is the death of his saints.
> O LORD, truly I am your servant;
>   I am your servant, the son of your maidservant;
>   you have freed me from my chains (116:15–16).

I suspect one of the most demoralizing things about this experience through which the psalmist had so recently passed, was to realize that his friends had proven to be of the fair-weather variety. They couldn't care less whether he lived or died. It must have been an immensely painful discovery: to be at the very threshold of the grave and be unsure whether anybody's going to miss you or mourn for you. To say the least, it is a savage blow to one's self-esteem. What a healing balm it must have been to discover that, alone though he was, he was not totally unloved or unwanted.

This intervention of God on his behalf proved that he was valued. Unworthy though he undoubtedly felt of such an honor, he discovered himself to be a child of God. The Lord would not lightly permit the death of one of his own; they are precious to him. What was it Jesus said? "Are not five sparrows sold for two pennies? Yet not one of them is forgotten by God. . . . Don't be afraid; you are worth more than many sparrows" (Luke 12:6–7).

God Wanted His Friendship

> For you, O LORD, have delivered my soul from death,
>   my eyes from tears,
>   my feet from stumbling,
>   that I may walk before the LORD
>   in the land of the living (116:8–9).

The expression *to walk before the Lord* has the idea of conducting one's life in God's intimate company. It is a phrase that was used of Abraham.

God didn't just deliver this man to satisfy some abstract moral principle. God had a personal interest in saving this man: he wanted to enjoy his fellowship. There is no discovery in the whole of the Bible that is more thrilling than that. Religion is not just a matter of how we feel about God; it is about how God feels about us. He cares about us, he values us, he wants our friendship. No wonder this man's heart was moved by this experience. A dangerous situation it may have been, but it had almost been worth it. For in answer to that desperate prayer, God had stepped in and showed this man things about himself that he would never have discovered otherwise. God wanted his friendship, and what could the man do but give it to him?

A Dedicated Life

Just for a moment, imagine you were on the boat that went down in the Thames. Imagine that you are a nonswimmer and feel yourself being dragged helplessly by the tide downriver. Just suppose one of those other guests, at great personal risk to his life, swims after you, grabs you by the collar, and drags you to safety. Wouldn't you feel like you wanted to express some appreciation to that person? Isn't it quite likely there might be a bottle of champagne waiting when he got home from the hospital? Indeed, would it be too much to say that as long as you lived, you would feel a debt of gratitude to that person for the way he had saved your life that day?

That's how the psalmist felt about God. He knew the peril he'd been in; he knew how close he'd come to death; he knew God didn't owe him anything; and yet in his love, God had rescued him. It was impossible in a situation like that not to ask the question, How can I repay the Lord for all his goodness to me?

Appropriation

> I will lift up the cup of salvation (116:13a).

Again, the translation is a little misleading because the verb just means "to pick up" rather than "to lift up." He isn't offering anything to God.

The psalmist is saying rather: "I'm not going to turn up my nose at God's salvation; I am going to pick it up. I am going to accept it gratefully and enthusiastically." That's how I can repay the Lord for his goodness to me.

Consecration

> I will lift up the cup of salvation
>> and call on the name of the LORD (116:13).

It was at that moment of crisis back in verse 4 that he tells us he had called on the name of the Lord, perhaps for the first time in his life. But gratitude demanded that he shouldn't continue to treat prayer as some kind of spiritual communication cord, for use in emergency only. This God had saved him so that he could walk before him, and that meant turning prayer from a fire alarm into a daily habit. He pledged himself to be a man of prayer.

Testimony

> I will fulfill my vows to the LORD
>> in the presence of all his people (116:14).

Notice the public emphasis in this commitment. In the closing verses he clarifies what he means by it:

> I will sacrifice a thank offering to you
>> and call on the name of the LORD.
> I will fulfill my vows to the LORD
>> in the presence of all his people,
> in the courts of the house of the LORD—
>> in your midst, O Jerusalem (116:17–19a).

In other words, for this psalmist, a public commitment to God meant going up to the temple in Jerusalem and testifying there in front of everybody, both by the sacrifice he offered and by the personal promises he made there, that he had pledged a new lifelong dedication to God.

I suspect that is why he wrote this psalm. Poet that he was, he decided that a song of worship ought to be sung on this occasion. He wanted everybody to know what had happened to him. He wanted everybody to know how he felt about it. Indeed, in a real sense this is not a psalm of devotion so much as a psalm of testimony.

There may be some readers who really empathize with this psalm, because there was a moment in their lives when they stood on the brink of death, too. I remember meeting a man in the hospital and reading this psalm to him. He had just gone through major heart surgery, and when I finished reading it to him, there were tears in his eyes, so powerfully and directly did it speak to him.

But I guess the majority of us would have to say that no such traumatic drama has yet punctuated our life's experience. We have never been seriously ill, never been involved in a serious road accident. The threshold of death is unexplored territory for us personally. I suppose that such readers may feel this psalm has less relevance to them for that reason. But if so, we could be very wrong.

Undoubtedly this psalm is of special application to anybody who has passed through a life-threatening crisis. But what you and I perhaps most need to grasp is that according to the Bible, whether we realize it or not, we are all in a life-threatening crisis, here and now. The deliverance the psalmist is talking about, a deliverance from a personal peril, is, in fact, a model of deliverance every single human being on the face of this earth needs to find. We, too, are in danger. We, too, need to be saved.

Part of the reason we don't realize that, of course, is that preachers often don't paint the picture of our human plight as they should. We imagine ourselves to be on board a pleasure cruiser, dancing to the disco. Everything in the world is OK. And God, in such a world, is an optional extra; his absence doesn't really disturb our pleasure. But that is not the truth of our human existence as the Bible sees it. The Bible says you and I are not, by nature, sitting on board a pleasure cruiser enjoying the music. On the contrary, we are in the water, thrashing against the tide. By nature, we are going to our death; by nature, we are under the judgment of God. That is the situation all of us are in. And make no mistake about it, it is a dangerous situation. Nobody spoke about the danger with more clarity than Jesus, who said: "Don't fear those who kill the body; fear him who, after he has killed, has power to cast into hell."

Jonathan Edwards, a great preacher of a previous century, caused great controversy by preaching a sermon called *Sinners in the Hands of an Angry God*. People didn't like it. "Let everyone who is without Christ," he said, "awaken and flee from the wrath to come." It was real old-fashioned hellfire and brimstone stuff. Yet I suggest to you, those are exactly the words we need to hear if we are to make any sense at all of what the Bible means when it says we need to be saved. It is little wonder we can't make sense of it, if there is nothing that we need to be saved from. People who are traveling along happily on the deck of the pleasure cruiser don't need to be saved; only those do who know themselves to be perishing in the water just as the psalmist did: "The cords of death entangled me . . . I was overcome by trouble and sorrow. Then I called on the name of the LORD: 'O LORD, save me!'" Only when we know our plight are words like that going to come to our lips.

The Pathway to Deliverance

We need to be saved, and the psalmist is telling us we can be. The pathway of our own experience of deliverance is identical to his. First, like him we need to recognize the dangerous situation we are in. If we don't feel the walls of hell closing in on us, it is doubtful whether we will be much moved to seek to escape from them. Then we need to turn to God, like him, in desperate prayer if need be: O Lord, save me. There is no examination to pass, no catechism to learn, no ritual to perform, no money to pay; all it requires is a cry of faith: I believed, therefore I spoke. In my trouble I had no one to hang on to except you, Lord, so I did. O Lord, save me! And it is then that we discover the divine initiative: when I was in great need, he saved me. On that Palestinian hillside, two thousand years ago, a cross stood silhouetted against an unnatural sky, and a Man cried: "My God, my God, why have you forsaken me?" The answer to that question is that we were in great need, and through that Man, God saved us: he was wounded for our transgressions; he was bruised for our iniquities. We, like simplehearted, foolish sheep, had gone astray, and the Lord laid on him the sin of us all.

In our helplessness there was nothing we could do ourselves, nor was there anything anybody else could do for us. God stepped in to provide his own deliverance. Why? For the same reason he stepped in to deliver this psalmist. Because he pitied us, because he valued us, but, most amazing of all, because he wanted our friendship. That is what he offers us.

Here is the cup of salvation, he says, pick it up. You want to know how you can repay me for all the goodness I have shown you? Then personally appropriate this salvation I have provided. Don't turn up your nose at a gift that has cost the blood of my Son. Own it as your own.

You say you want to do something more to pay the debt you owe me? Then become a man or woman of prayer. Stop using prayer like that communication cord whenever you are in trouble; start using prayer as a daily habit of fellowship with me. I want your friendship; I want you to start living each day in my company, walking before me.

You say: But I want to do something else, Lord, to repay you for all your goodness toward me. Well, there is a third thing: make a public commitment to me. Just like the psalmist did, don't keep this all to yourself. Don't lock it in the privacy of your own heart. Tell everybody else about it. Like the psalmist, make your vows to the Lord public, in the presence of all his people.

We may not have been on that pleasure cruiser that sank on the Thames, but whether we realize it or not, we are in a crisis situation: a moment of decision confronts us. What was it that young survivor said? "I just prayed to God." That's all the psalmist did. It is all any of us can do, but the tragedy of this life is that so many people never, sincerely, life-changingly, do it.

9

The Mystery of God

*A*lice was beginning to get very tired of sitting by her sister on the bank and of having nothing to do. Once or twice, she peeped into the book her sister was reading, but it had no pictures in it. 'What's the use of a book,' thought Alice, 'without pictures?'"

There are many adults who, if they were honest, would be inclined to agree with those opening sentiments of Lewis Carroll's *Alice in Wonderland*. Pictures are so much more compelling, so much more interesting than mere words. That's why every publisher employs illustrators; every newspaper, photographers. That's why television is so much more popular than radio and cinema than the public library. Perhaps that is why so many people profess to find the Bible difficult; for undoubtedly, the Bible is a book without pictures.

When it comes to the Bible, not only are the pictures absent, but they are strictly forbidden. "Thou shalt not make for thyself a graven image," says the second commandment. People have tried, of course. There is the story of the little boy painting a picture at school. "Tell me about it," said his teacher. "I am painting a picture of God," answered the juvenile Rembrandt. "But no one knows what God looks like," said the teacher. "They will when I've finished!" he replied.

He wasn't the first to display that kind of artistic self-assurance. In his great mural on the ceiling of the Sistine Chapel in Rome, Michelangelo depicts God the Creator as a kind of muscular geriatric, his long white hair and flowing beard attached rather incongruously to the body of an Olympic athlete. It is a masterpiece, but it is a picture that amply illustrates just why the Bible is so hostile to graven images. However great an artist you are, you can never do justice to God. There have been few painters in the history of human civilization who have had the genius of Michelangelo, but his portrait of the Creator makes him look like a Santa Claus on vitamin pills, and the damage that has been done to the religious consciousness of Western culture as a result of that picture and others like it is incalculable.

Martin Luther once said to Erasmus: "Erasmus, your thoughts of God are too human." So they were, and he would voice the same complaint at the vast majority of twentieth century men and women who have all been nourished, as Erasmus was, on the graven images of Renaissance humanism. Our God is too human. In fact, I suggest to you, there are still countless people today who, if they but knew it, have a mental image of God that is shaped, not by the Word of God, but by the paintings of Michelangelo.

The Bible is a book without pictures. It has to be. For the same reason, the tabernacle in the wilderness had to be a tent without windows: because there is an essential, impenetrable mystery about God. To try to paint a picture of God is presumptuously to dispel that mystery; it is to reduce the infinity of God to dimensions which, however impressive, are comprehensible to the human mind; and it is to represent the holiness of God by images which, however reverent, are familiar to the human mind. Such a truncated, ordinary God is God no longer. "To what will you liken God?" asks the prophet Isaiah. His challenge is unanswerable; we scan the universe in vain for adequate

Psalm 139

[1]O LORD, you have searched me
and you know me.
[2]You know when I sit and when I rise;
you perceive my thoughts from afar.
[3]You discern my going out and my lying
down;
you are familiar with all my ways.
[4]Before a word is on my tongue
you know it completely, O LORD.

[5]You hem me in—behind and before;
you have laid your hand upon me.
[6]Such knowledge is too wonderful for me,
too lofty for me to attain.

[7]Where can I go from your Spirit?
Where can I flee from your presence?
[8]If I go up to the heavens, you are there;
if I make my bed in the depths, you are
there.
[9]If I rise on the wings of the dawn,
if I settle on the far side of the sea,
[10]even there your hand will guide me,
your right hand will hold me fast.

[11]If I say, "Surely the darkness will hide me
and the light become night around me,"
[12]even the darkness will not be dark to
you;
the night will shine like the day,
for darkness is as light to you.

[13]For you created my inmost being;
you knit me together in my mother's
womb.
[14]I praise you because I am fearfully and
wonderfully made;

your works are wonderful,
I know that full well.
[15]My frame was not hidden from you
when I was made in the secret place.
When I was woven together in the
depths of the earth,
[16]your eyes saw my unformed body.
All the days ordained for me
were written in your book
before one of them came to be.

[17]How precious to me are your
thoughts, O God!
How vast is the sum of them!
[18]Were I to count them,
they would outnumber the grains of
sand.
When I awake,
I am still with you.

[19]If only you would slay the wicked,
O God!
Away from me, you bloodthirsty men!
[20]They speak of you with evil intent;
your adversaries misuse your name.
[21]Do I not hate those who hate you, O
LORD,
and abhor those who rise up against
you?
[22]I have nothing but hatred for them;
I count them my enemies.

[23]Search me, O God, and know my heart;
test me and know my anxious
thoughts.
[24]See if there is any offensive way in me,
and lead me in the way everlasting.

comparisons. No analogy will suffice to describe the being of God, and for that reason no canvas will suffice to contain him. He is incomparable, unfathomable, ineffable and therefore, essentially, invisible. He dwells, says the apostle Paul, in unapproachable light. No one has seen him; no one *can* see him.

The question we inevitably want to ask, confronted by a God who is so essentially invisible, is, of course: How then are we to form any valid idea of God? If the noblest efforts of our most gifted artists to portray him are to be dismissed as idolatrous caricatures, then how on earth can we, whose imaginations are so much inferior to theirs, possibly entertain thoughts worthy of the majesty of God? In the absence of visual images, how can God ever be anything to us but, to use a phrase coined by Churchill, a riddle, wrapped in a mystery, within an enigma?

The answer is *words*.

The Bible undoubtedly is a book without pictures, but when it comes to the being of God, the pen of the prophet can communicate what the brush of the artist must inevitably distort: the mystery of God. And nowhere does the Bible exhibit the power of words to do that more eloquently than in Psalm 139.

Many would regard this psalm as the most profound poem in all Hebrew literature. It is an intensely moving meditation on the nature of God. But note that it is a meditation pursued not by the veneration of visual images, but by reflection on the invisible attributes of God. David's God may be a mystery, but David knows what God is like, invisible though he is, and he tells us.

The psalm is constructed in four stanzas, six verses in each, with the first four verses of each stanza usually standing a little bit away from the last two of the six. In the first stanza, verses 1–6, we find David meditating on the mystery of God's all-embracing knowledge. In the second stanza, in verses 7–12, he turns to the mystery of God's inescapable presence. In stanza 3, verses 13–18, he reflects on the mystery of God's sovereign providence. Then in the final stanza, verses 19–24, David presents to us the ultimate choice with which this God of mystery confronts us: we can either be hostile rebels against him, or his willing servants. That is the spiritual challenge of the mystery of God.

God's All-Embracing Knowledge

> O LORD, you have searched me
>   and you know me.
> You know when I sit and when I rise;
>   you perceive my thoughts from afar.
> You discern my going out and my lying down;
>   you are familiar with all my ways.
> Before a word is on my tongue
>   you know it completely, O LORD.
>
> You hem me in—behind and before;
>   you have laid your hand upon me.
> Such knowledge is too wonderful for me,
>   too lofty for me to attain (139:1–6).

Just like those remote-controlled security cameras in supermarkets, David feels himself under inspection by a similar all-seeing eye. But in his case the surveillance is unceasing, and it scrutinizes his mind as well as his actions. Not only is his every movement chronicled by God, but his inmost thoughts are also read, his half-formed words are anticipated. And that, not by a mere passive receptor of information like a spy-satellite, but by a master-detective who snoops like some insatiable busybody into every detail of his existence, armed with X-ray cameras and laser probes. "You have searched me," he says. "You know me. I have no privacy, no room in the palace from which I can exclude you, no corner of my mind that I can bolt the door and bar you entry from. Everything I do, everything I say, everything I think, is wide open to your gaze." Some would feel tyrannized by such uninvited interference. Like the characters in Orwell's *1984*, they would be oppressed by the constant reminder that Big Brother is watching them.

Interestingly, David doesn't see it that way. True, some commentators do want to interpret verse 5 as if David feels trapped and is complaining of God's inquisitorial tactics: "You hem me in—behind and before; you have laid your hand upon me." It is as if David is saying, "Everywhere I go you shadow me; every step I take, I feel you breathing down my neck." But I am not at all sure that is David's intention in this verse. Though that verb translated here "you hem me in" can

147

be rendered as "you besiege me," which has a hostile flavor to it, it can also be rendered "you guard me" or "you encircle me for my protection." I think that is David's meaning here.

This all-embracing knowledge of God is not an ominous threat to him. It is a welcome refuge. That is the only way we can explain why he goes on to say in verse 6: "Such knowledge is too wonderful for me, too lofty for me to attain." As he consults his feelings about this all-knowing character of God, his reaction is one, not of resentment, but of grateful wonder at a divine intelligence that totally eclipses anything of which his feeble human intellect is capable. "I freely confess," says David, "that I cannot understand you, God. You are a mystery to me, and ironically the more I find out about you, the more awesome, the more amazing, the more mysterious, you become."

God's Inescapable Presence

> Where can I go from your Spirit?
>> Where can I flee from your presence?
> If I go up to the heavens, you are there;
>> if I make my bed in the depths, you are there.
> If I rise on the wings of the dawn,
>> if I settle on the far side of the sea,
> even there your hand will guide me,
>> your right hand will hold me fast (139:7–10).

It does seem as if, at least as a fleeting hypothesis, David here considers the idea of flight—flight from those irresistible, all-penetrating eyes of God. He wonders if there is somewhere in the universe where he can escape God and be alone. But merely to entertain that thought is immediately to perceive its impossibility. This mysterious God not only knows everything, but he is everywhere. "Why," he says, "I could take a rocket ship and blast up into the stratosphere, but I'd never outdistance you. I'd find you up there waiting for me when I arrived. I could, like some Greek hero, cross the ferry of death and descend into the terrifying depths of the underworld; but I'd never elude you. Even there you would still be present. I could take the swiftest supersonic jet plane and race the light of the rising sun as it

148

sweeps across the continent, even to the remotest corners of the earth. But I'd never outpace you even with the wings of dawn on my back. On the contrary, I'd find, like Jonah, that you are just as powerful there as you are here. No matter how far I go, no matter how fast I travel, no matter what direction I choose, you are inescapable, God."

Once again it would be very easy to resent that. Like the ubiquitous bad penny, God always turns up. Many have echoed David's words in verse 7 with tones of frustration in their voices: "Where can I go from your Spirit? Where can I flee from your presence?" I want to get away from you, God. But once again, a careful reading of this psalm doesn't suggest to me that that is what David is saying. He isn't trying to run away; if he contemplates the idea at all, it is only to dismiss it as an undesirable option which is out of the question anyway. No, David's reaction to God's inescapable presence is the same as his reaction to God's all-embracing knowledge: one of gratitude. No matter what happens to me, I can always rely on your being there—not to threaten me, but to direct me; not to make me feel anxious, but to make me feel secure. "Even there your hand will guide me, your right hand will hold me fast." And if we are right to interpret David's mood in that way, it is clear that verse 11 should not be read as some translations do, as if it were a last-ditch, desperate darting of the eyes in search of some way of escape. Verse 11 is rather an answer to the fleeting fear that crosses David's mind that maybe there is some situation after all in which he could lose this precious assurance of God's presence in his life.

> If I say, "Surely the darkness will hide me
>   and the light become night around me,"
> even the darkness will not be dark to you;
>   the night will shine like the day,
>   for darkness is as light to you (139:11–12).

David is anticipating here the possibility that in some moment of panic, in a desperate situation, he might find himself saying: Help! The lights have all gone out; God cannot see me anymore. I am deserted by him; he has forgotten me. "But," says David, "even if in some extremity of depression, I was brought to such a pitch of despair, I would be wrong. For no matter how dark the situation seems to my eyes, God has infrared vision; he sees in the night as he sees in the day. His reassuring hand, therefore, is just as reliable in adversity as it is in prosperity." One recalls those famous words quoted by King George VI, "Put your hand in the hand of God. That will be better than light and safer than a known way." God is always there; it is impossible that he should not be there. He is the inescapable God. "Even though I walk through the valley of the shadow of death, I will fear no evil, for you are with me" (Ps. 23:4a).

God's Sovereign Providence

> For you created my inmost being;
>   you knit me together in my mother's womb.
> I praise you because I am fearfully and wonderfully made;
>   your works are wonderful,
>   I know that full well.
> My frame was not hidden from you
>   when I was made in the secret place.
> When I was woven together in the depths of the earth,
>   your eyes saw my unformed body.
> All the days ordained for me
>   were written in your book
>   before one of them came to be.
>
> How precious to me are your thoughts, O God!
>   How vast is the sum of them!
> Were I to count them,
>   they would outnumber the grains of sand.
> When I awake,
>   I am still with you (139:13–18).

If anything deserves to be called a mystery, then the birth of a child does. The psalmist, of course, knew nothing of the details of human genetics and embryology that our twentieth-century medical science has unraveled. He'd never heard of DNA or chromosomes; he'd never seen the pulsing heart of a living fetus on an ultrasound scan. In fact, I personally doubt he had ever witnessed the delivery of a baby, because in most primitive societies men are kept well out of the way on such occasions.

But David knew enough biology to be amazed that something as complicated as a human being could be put together in nine months inside a woman's uterus. And he knew enough theology to know that there was only one credible explanation of this amazing miracle of life: the sovereign providence of God. "You created me," he said, "like a potter shaping a vessel. You knit me together like a weaver blending together threads in a complex tapestry. If there was ever a time when I was concealed in the darkness, out of your divine line of sight, then surely, God, it was during that antenatal period of my existence. In those early days, I was lost in obscurity; my own mother wasn't aware of my existence for a while. It was as if I was buried in some deep cave under the earth, cut off from all external light and communication. But astonishingly," he says, "it was precisely then, when I didn't even exist as far as the world at large was concerned, that I was most conspicuously the recipient of your care and attention. You saw me there. I wasn't hidden from you at all. Indeed, even before that embryo that was me matured enough to be recognizable as a human form, you had my life planned for me, from start to finish. 'All the days ordained for me were written in your book before one of them came to be.'"

Once again, it is not hard to imagine someone taking umbrage at such a strong doctrine of the sovereign control that God exercises over the whole of the human life. It smacks of predestination of a particularly vicious kind. This is a God who creates a life, superintending every detail of its development, every trait of its genetic code, every incident of its intrauterine experience, every moment of its subsequent allotted lifespan. All things are irrevocably fixed, written in indelible ink in some heavenly ledger as by the remorseless finger of Omar Khayyam. Where is the freedom in that? I am just a pawn on God's cosmic chessboard. But again, though David could have taken such an attitude, in fact, his reaction to the role of God's sovereign providence in his life is one of gratitude and worship: "I praise you because I am fearfully and wonderfully made" (v. 14). "There is something awesome about this human psyche of mine," he says. "No one really understands me. I don't really understand myself. But you do, God. You comprehend every nut and every bolt of my physical and emotional makeup, for you designed it in the first place. You know me inside out." If you repoint the Hebrew text, that is exactly what he says in verse 14: not, "I know that full well," but "you know me full well."

For David there is something immensely moving, immensely touching about this sovereign providence of God in his life. He tells us in verse 17: "How precious to me are your thoughts, O God!" In context, the thoughts he has in mind are all those prenatal plans that God made for him. There were so many details to be decided: thousands upon thousands, millions upon millions of separate pieces of information required to specify this vast, complex, biophysical, psychosomatic, self-conscious being which was David. "And," says David, "you took a personal interest in every line of the program: my height, my eye color, my IQ, my fear of spiders, my infantile trauma, my childhood accidents, my adolescent trials, my adult achievements, my relationships, my illnesses, my strengths, my weaknesses. Why," says David, "if I were to try to enumerate all the things which you, in your sovereign providence, have organized on my behalf, it would be a better soporific than counting sheep. For they are more in number than the grains of sand on the seashore. Even when I woke up, the counting would have to go on, because your thoughts about me never stop; you are adding new entries to the list all the time. Every new day that dawns finds your sovereign providence still at work, directing the course of my life." Some may find that sovereign providence a threat to their human freedom. Says David, "I find it an immensely precious comfort in all my human vulnerability."

The Spiritual Challenge

If only you would slay the wicked, O God!
    Away from me, you bloodthirsty men!
They speak of you with evil intent;
    your adversaries misuse your name.
Do I not hate those who hate you, O LORD,
    and abhor those who rise up against you?
I have nothing but hatred for them;
    I count them my enemies.

> Search me, O God, and know my heart;
>   test me and know my anxious thoughts.
> See if there is any offensive way in me,
>   and lead me in the way everlasting (139:19–24).

I don't know whether David really fell asleep while he was writing verse 18; but if he did, then certainly in verse 19 he has been very rudely awakened.

His devotional meditations on God in his quiet time have had to give way now to the harsh realities of his political career. It is time to get up, face the office, or in David's case, the royal court again. All around him in that court he is aware of intrigue and corruption, of godless, violent men, intent on evil, who scorn the moral sensitivity of a man who, like him, speaks of God. He knows he has a choice as he comes out of his quiet time that morning. In a very real sense it is the ultimate choice. Either he must identify with these ruthless men and their unscrupulous ways, or he must find the courage to be different. He must stand out from them as a man of principles, standard of godliness, and integrity in a situation where the vast majority of people hold such things in contempt. In this closing stanza he tells us what his choice was. "I have decided," he says, "to put God before my personal popularity, perhaps even before my personal safety. I have decided to distance myself from these evil men in my court. I have decided to let it be known that I do not approve of their tactics; and even if I am politically powerless to prevent them carrying out their wicked schemes, I pray God's judgment will fall on them. I refuse to number them among my allies.

"For unlike them, I worship an invisible God—a God who searches my every thought, my every motive, my every deed; a God from whom I cannot escape; and yet a God upon whom I daily rely for my very breath. I praise him for his providential care of me; I am grateful to him for his unceasing presence in my life; I welcome his all-seeing investigation of my heart. Search me, O God. I know you have searched me, but I want you to know, God, that I am willing to be searched. 'Search me, O God, and know my heart; test me and know my anxious thoughts.' Of course, they are anxious thoughts. Who ever invited the almighty God into his heart without feeling anxious about it! But enter there, and see if there is any offensive way in me, and lead me in the way everlasting."

There are all kinds of applications that are suggested to one's mind as we reflect on this psalm. We have already spoken of the immense importance of the psalm theologically. If you turn to works of systematic theology, there will always be a sizeable piece dedicated to the exposition of this psalm. It is a key text in the Old Testament's doctrine of God, ranking only with Isaiah 40.

This psalm has also become very important in the field of social ethics in recent years. Verses 13–16 have enormous relevance to the debate about abortion and embryo research. A fundamental ethical question that has to be resolved in regard to those debates is the status of an unborn child: When does a fetus become a human being? Down through the centuries people have often tried to identify the point in the development of an embryo when it ceases to be part of the woman's body and becomes a new human individual.

Speculation began with Aristotle, who suggested that the fetus became truly human when it was quickened in the womb. But we know now that quickening is simply a matter of degree. The fetus is moving all the time. The quickening is simply when the mother becomes aware of it. More recently, people have talked about the viability of the fetus outside the womb as the key criterion, but with the advances in obstetric care of premature babies, fetuses are surviving from earlier and earlier in the pregnancy.

It is not the purpose of this book to delve into this extremely complex subject. But it is significant that we find a man here, looking back under the inspiration of God to the very beginnings of his personal existence. And you will notice he traces that existence, not to the moment of birth, not to some moment of viability, not to some moment of quickening. He seems to trace it all the way back to the moment of conception. "You created my inmost being; you knit me together in my mother's womb." Though not yet self-conscious, already as an embryo he perceives he is that person who will one day look back and say, "That was me." Though just a fetus he was the product of God's creative skills. He was the recipient of God's antenatal care. Already in the womb, God had a plan for his life. It is hard to see how anybody who accepts David's view of his own existence can possibly justify treating a fetus as a part of the mother's body which, like an appendix or a gall bladder, she can choose to remove. God's Word here seems to speak so plainly of the human identity of the unborn child. Psalm 139 is a vital and moving Scripture if for no other reason than for the assurance it gives to us of the value of prenatal life.

A Personal Challenge

But it is the very personal challenge that concludes the psalm that has the most relevance for me: "Search me, O God." Years ago, before I became a Christian, with the exception perhaps of the writings of Agatha Christie, I didn't have much time for mysteries. Christians, it seemed to me, always resorted to mystery when their brains failed them. Time and time again I thought I had a Christian friend pinned up against the wall, metaphorically speaking, by the unanswerable logic of my atheism. The inconsistent and contradictory nature of his faith was plain for all to see, and the moment had surely come when at last honesty demanded that he would admit it. But always he slithered out of my grasp, through the same unsatisfactory loophole: "Oh well, what you have got to realize, Roy, is that there is a lot of mystery about God; we cannot possibly understand it all."

It did not matter what aspect of Christian doctrine we were discussing—the Trinity, predestination, the problem of suffering, the incarnation, the end of the world—the conversation always ended in his recourse to mystery and mine to frustration. "Mystery," I said. "Mystery is just a get-out clause. Mystery is just a religious euphemism for absurdity. Agatha Christie's mysteries I can appreciate because they are always solved, but talking to a Christian is like following Miss Marple all the way through the book only to discover that the final chapter has been ripped out! If you believe in mysteries, you will believe in anything—the Loch Ness monster, the Abominable Snowman, flying saucers—what are they all but unsolved mysteries? If I were prepared to accept 'mystery' as an answer to my intellectual quest, I'd still believe in the Tooth Fairy!"

No, I wasn't very fond of mysteries. But I can remember the day when for the very first time I read this psalm. That was the day I realized that I couldn't dispense with mystery if I ever wanted to know

God. I realized that it is an inevitable condition of all true and lasting admiration that the object of that admiration should be greater than our knowledge of it. The growth of our knowledge of that object of admiration, far from touching the limits of its marvelousness, should more and more convince us of the inaccessibility of those limits of wonder. David showed me that; he showed me that a God I could fully understand would not be a God I would be able to worship. Worship is awe at that which surpasses the understanding. To worship is to bow and say, "Such knowledge is too wonderful for me, too lofty for me to attain."

Psalm 139 taught me what I suppose is really glaringly obvious to many, that if ever I wanted to experience God, I would have to come to terms with mystery. Maybe you do too.

All the way through this psalm we have seen that people can have two quite opposite reactions to the wonder of this invisible and mysterious God. On the one hand, it is quite possible to rebel against such a God, to resent his omniscience as a hostile invasion of our privacy, to flee his all-pervasive presence and seek some place in the universe unthreatened by his nosiness. It is possible to deny his sovereign providence over our lives and assert, instead, our autonomous human freedom. Make no mistake about it, there are many people who do just that. Sometimes they do so quite deliberately by adopting an atheistic creed. But not always. No, some people, though they are hostile against the God of the Bible, would never say so. Indeed, such people may well feel perfectly at home with some ideas of God. They may well stand, bathed in admiration at the Sistine Chapel and that masterpiece of Michelangelo's. After all, they say to themselves, there must be someone who got the world going in the first place, mustn't there? And that kind of heavenly grandfather who leaves us alone most of the time, but is always there to call up if we are in a spot, that is a perfectly acceptable picture of the Creator. Nobody objects to a God like that.

But this mysterious, unfathomable God of Psalm 139 is different. He won't allow us to reduce him to a nice comfortable size or a nice familiar shape; he insists on transcending our human imagination every time. That sort of God is disturbing. You can't control a God like that; you can't keep him in his place. He challenges us. He challenges our consciences with that all-embracing knowledge of his, insisting on unmasking all those ugly hidden things we'd really rather keep to ourselves. He challenges our complacency, popping up in that infuriatingly ubiquitous way without any invitation at all when we really thought we'd gotten rid of him. Most of all, he challenges our independence, insisting that we are not in control of our lives in the way we like to make out—he is.

If that is where you are with God at the moment, you have a choice to make. Maybe you are not an atheist, but have you really come to terms with the God of the Bible? Psalm 139 assures you and me that we cannot escape from him. We may try—I remember trying for many months—but it is a futile quest. There is no place in this universe where you can hide from this God. Perhaps you are familiar with Francis Thompson's great poem, *The Hound of Heaven*. I suspect it was inspired by the second stanza of the psalm:

> I fled Him, down the nights, and down the days;
> I fled Him, down the arches of the years;
> I fled Him, down the labyrinthine ways
> Of my own mind, and in the mist of tears
> I hid from Him, and under running laughter.
> Up vistaed hopes I sped;
> And shot, precipitated,
> Adown Titanic glooms of chasmed fears,
> From those strong Feet that followed, followed after.

It is, as David says, the mystery of God's inescapable presence. "Where can I go from your Spirit? Where can I flee from your presence?" No matter how determined we are to shut God out of our lives, he will not go away. We may turn from the road because we see him up ahead, but at the end of the path he'll be there waiting for us; he is that kind of God.

We can't escape him, and if we had any sense, we wouldn't want to. For he is not the interfering and oppressive tyrant we fear. He is our Creator. He cared for us long before we knew we existed. He watches over us, not to crush our independence, but because he loves us. He has a whole file of notes in his heavenly memory bank just about us and each one personally dictated. Why do we run away from him? Why do we shut the door so firmly in his face? Don't we know this great God of mystery wants to save us? "To lead [us] in the way everlasting"?

For all the sublime heights of this psalm, there is one mystery about God that David never knew and that he was never able to include in his meditations as a result. But for the Christian, it is the greatest mystery of all: the mystery of Bethlehem, the mystery of Calvary. I said that the Bible is a book without pictures, and so it is. And that is why the incarnation is so spellbindingly wonderful. If Jesus had come to us from the pages of Greek mythology or Eastern mysticism, there would have been no mystery about him. Those religions are used to pictures of God; their deities are all too human. But Jesus comes to us out of the pages of the Bible, a book without pictures, a book that prohibits pictures, a book that insists upon the invisibility of God and therefore cannot speak of Jesus without paradox, without mystery.

God dwells in unapproachable light, writes Paul. Yet Jesus is the image of the invisible God. No one has ever seen God, says John. Yet he who has seen Jesus has seen the Father. Is there any way of understanding that, without resort to mystery? And the greatest mystery of all is that God so loved this world of ours, sinners though we are, that he sent his Son that we might find the way everlasting.

So why are we so reluctant to invite him in? Why are we so churlish as to stay with those who reject this God, who hate this God?

David shows us the way here to real fulfillment of our human existence when he says, "Search me, O God." In one respect, it is accepting the inevitable, for what God discovers when he searches us is no surprise to him; he's already looked there before. The reason he longs for us to pray this prayer is not because there is something hidden inside us that he doesn't know about, but because he wants our friendship. He wants a relationship with us that will enable him to cleanse us from every offensive way and lead us in the way everlasting.

10

THE WORD OF PRAISE

*I*t is said that there are three words that are understood in every language on the face of the globe: *Amen, Alleluia,* and *Coca Cola.* In this chapter we are going to be looking at the second of that trio, *Alleluia.*

Alleluia is a Hebrew word, in fact a fusion of two Hebrew words: *Hallelu* is an imperative meaning "praise ye," and *Yah,* that suffix on the end, is a contraction of the name for God, Jehovah. So *Alleluia* means "praise ye the Lord." In Old Testament times it was often used as a liturgical response in worship; in fact, any who come from a Church of England background will be familiar with this. In the old prayerbook the minister would say, "Praise ye the Lord," and the people were required to answer, "The Lord's name be praised."

Something very similar went on in the Jewish temple. Exchanges of this sort between priest and people were a common part of their order of service. Sometimes these responses were actually formalized and printed in their hymnbook, that is, the Book of Psalms.

And if you examine the five concluding songs in the Psalter, you'll see that each is a case in point. Each of these psalms begins and ends with the same liturgical refrain, Alleluia. You could say these five psalms constitute a kind of biblical equivalent of the "Alleluia Chorus," for this word of praise keeps recurring again and again.

However, the psalmist is not content that the congregation of God's people should just repeat this great word of praise, Alleluia, as some trite jingle. Still less, does he use Alleluia as a mantra to be chanted like Hare Krishna in order to artificially work up some state of spiritual ecstasy. He sets these Alleluias as parentheses, enclosing songs which are very rich in theological content. In fact, you could regard Alleluia in each case as a kind of liturgical alarm signal to the sluggish in the congregation. Alleluia, you've got be alert; you've got to wake up; there's business in hand, praising the Lord.

Praising the Lord isn't something you can do in a state of mindless euphoria; it requires the engagement of all your faculties. Alleluia is a poetic exclamation mark!

In confirmation of that, each of these psalms, having summoned the audience's attention by that opening shout, proceeds to recite, in different ways and with different emphases, the reasons the people of God have for praising the Lord: reasons associated with who he is and what he has done. So when you get to that final Alleluia at the end of each psalm, it isn't, as Alleluia sometimes is in our modern choruses, just a vacuous formula. It is a testimony to the commitment of the congregation to this God whom they have been describing in their song and to all the delight and joy they feel at knowing him.

The essence of biblical worship is that God has revealed himself. The only reason we can worship God is that we know something about him. As a result of his self-revelation, we have learned something about him that excites our admiration, our gratitude, our faith, our joy; and worship is the expression of that faith, that admiration, that gratitude, that joy.

Worship is a heartfelt, emotionally charged expression; but it is also a rational and thoughtful expression. True worship is always a response to what we know of God, as a result of his revealing himself to us.

160

These five concluding psalms in many respects are a kind of paradigm of that biblical understanding of what praise and worship is really all about. Alleluia isn't, in these psalms, just a buzzword. Inside each of these Alleluia sandwiches, if we may call them that, there is meat which gives substance to that "Praise the Lord" with which each psalm begins and ends. It is that meat in the sandwich that I want to unpack in this chapter, so that at the end of our study, we too, like the psalmist, will be able to praise the Lord in an intelligent way, in a way that engages not just our hearts but our minds as well.

God's Faithfulness to the Weak (Ps. 146)

I remember when I first came to Cambridge, I met an American student who expressed to me the disillusionment with leadership that he felt was rife in his society at the time. He put it to me like this: "We

---

Psalm 146

¹Praise the LORD.

Praise the LORD, O my soul.
² I will praise the LORD all my life;
I will sing praise to my God as long as
I live.

³Do not put your trust in princes,
in mortal men, who cannot save.
⁴When their spirit departs, they return
to the ground;
on that very day their plans come to
nothing.

⁵Blessed is he whose help is the God of
Jacob,
whose hope is in the LORD his God,
⁶the Maker of heaven and earth,
the sea, and everything in them—

the LORD, who remains faithful
forever.
⁷He upholds the cause of the oppressed
and gives food to the hungry.
The LORD sets prisoners free,
⁸ the LORD gives sight to the blind,
the LORD lifts up those who are bowed
down,
the LORD loves the righteous.
⁹The LORD watches over the alien
and sustains the fatherless and the
widow,
but he frustrates the ways of the
wicked.

¹⁰The LORD reigns forever,
your God, O Zion, for all generations.

Praise the LORD.

---

used to trust the generals, but Vietnam changed all that. We used to trust the politicians, but Watergate changed all that. We used to trust the scientists, but Three Mile Island changed all that. We used to trust the economists, but recession changed all that. Now we know there is no one to trust." He said that the sixties had been years of rebellion with student riots and demonstrations; the seventies had been years of apathy with flower power and gurus; and the eighties had been years of cynicism, because we believed there was no one to trust. I suspect this past decade has, generally speaking, proved his assessment true. This century of ours that came in on a rising tide of optimism about the perfectibility of the human race is going out with a sinking pessimism about the intractability of the problems that the human race faces.

Perhaps it is a comfort to know that the psalmist, though he lived two and a half millennia ago, was no stranger to these feelings of betrayed hope and bitter disappointment. Clearly, the people that he had looked to for leadership, the people he calls here *princes,* had let him down. But then, as he reflects on that, he comes to the conclusion that really it is only to be expected. No matter how noble their birth, no matter how prodigious their gifts, human beings are, after all, only human beings.

I am reminded of Archbishop Grindal's words to Queen Elizabeth I. He felt he had to rebuke his sovereign lady for her dictatorial attitude: "Remember, Madam," he said, "you are a mortal creature." Apparently, Queen Elizabeth was not amused by this; she heartily objected to being called a mortal creature even by an archbishop. But of course she was, in spite of her royal crown.

So are they all: Clinton and Yeltsin, Major and Kohl. Whichever prince of the twentieth century we put our hope in for a better tomorrow, I fear we may end up in disillusionment or even cynicism, for they are all mortal creatures. What was it God said to Adam? "You are made of the dust and to dust you shall return." Our psalmist recalls that divine curse in verse 4 and observes the shadow of futility it casts over all political ambition. "On that very day," he says, "their plans come to nothing." No matter how long the obituary, no matter how prestigious the funeral, no matter how large the estate, the paths of glory lead but to the grave.

162

That's why the psalmist's advice here has lost none of its relevance in the passing of two and a half thousand years. There is only one person in this world worthy of unconditional trust, and it isn't a mortal. "Do not put your trust in princes," he says, "in mortal men, who cannot save." There is only one person in this world you can depend upon: "Blessed is he whose help is the God of Jacob, whose hope is in the LORD his God . . . the LORD, who remains faithful forever."

As he goes on to explain in this psalm, if the weak of the earth are seeking a champion, someone to protect them in their vulnerability, someone to deliver them from their fears, they should forget the generals, forget the politicians, forget the scientists, forget the economists, for they are broken reeds, all of them.

The LORD, is the only one you can really rely on: "He upholds the cause of the oppressed and gives food to the hungry."

He is the only one you can rely on to fulfill his manifesto pledges to emancipate those who are in bondage: "The LORD, sets prisoners free, the LORD, gives sight to the blind."

He is the only one you can rely on to vindicate those whose minds and spirits have been broken by injustice: "The LORD, lifts up those who are bowed down, the LORD, loves the righteous."

He is the only one you can rely on to solve the problem of the refugees and the one-parent families: "The LORD, watches over the alien and sustains the fatherless and the widow."

He is the only one you can rely on at the end of the day to thwart the malice of those who abuse their power to exploit the weak: "He frustrates the ways of the wicked."

Some will say that these are just platitudes. Look at the real world. It's not like that, is it? Wickedness and injustice are rife on all sides. What possible grounds can the psalmist have for these bland confidences of his? The answer, of course, lies in his faith. He is speaking here about a God who had revealed himself: the Creator God (v. 6)— the Maker of heaven and earth, the Covenant God (v. 5)—the God of Jacob, the Sovereign God (v. 10)—the Lord who reigns forever.

If you believe, as this psalmist did, that this world is in the hands of such a God, you can have hope. In spite of all the injustice, in spite of all the misery, in spite of all the unsolved problems the human race faces, you can have hope. For this God can be depended upon: He "remains faithful forever" (v. 6). You may have to exercise patience, but you do not have to give way to despair if you believe the world is in the hands of such a God.

On the other hand, if you don't believe this world is in the hands of a God like that, you have no alternative but to despair. Cynicism is your only recourse, because you can be sure that mortal man can't save us. In this century of ours, a century stained by the blood of man's inhumanity to man, perhaps more gruesomely than any century that has preceded it, even the humanists are beginning to admit the fact.

Whether you can say Alleluia, echoing the psalmist's notes of joy, depends first and foremost on whether you are a believer. That, of course, has to be a very individual matter. It was for this psalmist; notice how he begins Psalm 146:

Praise the LORD.

Praise the LORD, O my soul.
I will praise the LORD all my life;
   I will sing praise to my God as long as I live (146:1–2).

Notice the first person pronouns, *my* and *I.* It is a very strong, personal emphasis. When this man says, "The LORD remains faithful forever," he is not just reciting a creed. Alleluia is no mere liturgical cant for him. It is a confession born of a deep personal commitment. "I will praise the LORD all my life." True praise and worship has to be like that; it can never be secondhand. Have you heard the story of the radio announcer who introduced the Sunday service one morning by saying, "Good morning, listeners, today's worship is a repeat of last Sunday's broadcast"? Some people come to church in just that manner, expecting that today's worship will be a repeat of last Sunday's. It is just mindless ritual. But it won't do. To put a loop of magnetic tape on the recorder so it keeps on saying "Alleluia, praise the Lord, Alleluia, praise the Lord," that isn't worship! There has to be this personal commitment to God, this personal faith in him, out of which our worship and praise flow. Only those can say Alleluia who can also say, I know this God remains faithful forever, and I trust him.

164

God's Special Love for His People (Ps. 147)

In Psalm 146, the psalmist speaks very generally of God's concern for justice in the world, and in Psalm 147 that same theme of God's common grace is still very evident. He speaks a lot, for instance, of God's providential care in nature. In verses 8–9 he attributes the fertility of the soil to God's hand. In verses 15–18 he speaks of how God

---

Psalm 147

¹Praise the LORD.

How good it is to sing praises to our God,
how pleasant and fitting to praise him!

²The LORD builds up Jerusalem;
he gathers the exiles of Israel.
³He heals the brokenhearted
and binds up their wounds.

⁴He determines the number of the stars
and calls them each by name.
⁵Great is our Lord and mighty in power;
his understanding has no limit.
⁶The LORD sustains the humble
but casts the wicked to the ground.

⁷Sing to the LORD with thanksgiving;
make music to our God on the harp.
⁸He covers the sky with clouds;
he supplies the earth with rain
and makes grass grow on the hills.
⁹He provides food for the cattle
and for the young ravens when they call.

¹⁰His pleasure is not in the strength of
the horse,
nor his delight in the legs of a man;

¹¹the LORD delights in those who fear him,
who put their hope in his unfailing
love.

¹²Extol the LORD, O Jerusalem;
praise your God, O Zion,
¹³for he strengthens the bars of your
gates
and blesses your people within you.
¹⁴He grants peace to your borders
and satisfies you with the finest of
wheat.

¹⁵He sends his command to the earth;
his word runs swiftly.
¹⁶He spreads the snow like wool
and scatters the frost like ashes.
¹⁷He hurls down his hail like pebbles.
Who can withstand his icy blast?
¹⁸He sends his word and melts them;
he stirs up his breezes, and the waters
flow.

¹⁹He has revealed his word to Jacob,
his laws and decrees to Israel.
²⁰He has done this for no other nation;
they do not know his laws.

Praise the LORD.

---

controls the weather and the seasons. But if you look carefully you will see that in this psalm, these general blessings of God which are evidenced toward all his creation are just a backdrop against which the psalmist wants to draw attention to the very special love that God has for his own people, for Jerusalem, for Israel.

Thus while it is generally true that God heals the brokenhearted (v. 3), it is especially true that God gathers the exiles of Israel to himself (v. 2). While it is generally true that God provides food for animals and the human race (v. 9), his real pleasure is not in the physical vigor of a horse or a man (v. 10); his special delight is in those who fear him, and who put their hope in his unfailing love (v. 11).

It is true that God controls the weather and simply has to utter his sovereign word to bring hailstones down from the heavens (vv. 17–18). Yet there is a very special ministry of that sovereign word which is reserved not for hailstones or air currents, but for the direction and guidance of his chosen people (vv. 19–20).

In every case, the psalmist is moving from the evidence of God's general love to his special love, and that's why he says in verses 12–14:

> Extol the LORD, O Jerusalem;
> praise your God, O Zion,
> for he strengthens the bars of your gates
> and blesses your people within you.
> He grants peace to your borders
> and satisfies you with the finest of wheat.

I suppose that may sound a bit like favoritism, but it isn't so. Israel did enjoy special blessings, but they were matched very precisely with special responsibilities. When Israel failed to obey the sovereign word that the Lord had revealed to her, she experienced judgment from God, far more severe than the pagan nations around her. Anyone who thinks that God showed partiality toward the Jews has not read those tortured passages in the Old Testament which speak of the devastation of Jerusalem. Indeed, anyone who thinks that God is partial toward the Jews has not seen the photos from Auschwitz. The Jews have paid heavily for their special privilege; scarcely can we call it favoritism. Israel was never God's pampered pet, and neither is the church.

166

In every age the people of God are his chosen vehicle for carrying his purpose into the world. As a result of that they are the recipients of special privileges. They know his Word, while others who do not have the Bible must languish in spiritual ignorance. But then they have a responsibility to obey that Word. They can enjoy security and satisfaction in their covenant relation to him that is not accessible to others who do not have such a personal relationship with God. They can, when they fall under judgment, experience his restoring and healing grace in a way that is unknown to others who have not learned the path of repentance and faith.

But the purpose of their being the people of God is to teach others that path. The purpose of their enjoying a covenant relationship is to welcome others into that same relationship. The people of God exist for the sake of the world around them. For that reason they have a special obligation to praise the Lord. This debt of gratitude that they owe him they must make public; they must proclaim his glory and his goodness. This great God, who numbers the stars, has chosen them, the humblest of the earth, to be his own. They, more than anybody else then, have grounds to say Alleluia. He has revealed his Word to them, and their mission is to "declare the praises of him who called [them] out of darkness into his wonderful light" (1 Peter 2:9).

That is very important for us to grasp if we would be worshipers. If the first thing you must decide, if you want to praise God, is whether you are a believer or not, the second thing you must come to terms with is whether or not God loves you. I am not speaking of his general love for all humanity; we know he loves the world. I mean, are you conscious that God loves you in a special way? Because if you are a believer, he does. Long before he made the world, he had you in his mind. You are special to him. He has worked in your life in a very individual and personalized way, because he has a special love for you. Those who feel that, praise him. How can they do anything else?

The question believing people often ask is, *Why me?* It seems so unfair, when others are allowed to plunge on in their reckless way to hell, he has arrested me and drawn me to his side; when others are allowed to remain in their spiritual blindness, he opened my eyes; when others are allowed to remain in the despair of their unbelief, somehow, by some miracle, he quickened faith in me. *Why me?* Every child of God asks that question. It is natural to ask it. We are meant to ask it. But there is no answer to it. Immediately you try to find a reason for God's special love directed to his people, and invariably you create a false religion. He loves me because I am a better person than others. He loves me because I decided to believe in him, unlike others. He loves me because I go to church, I've been baptized, and I read the Bible. No, his love is not a response to any of these things. The Bible gives us no reason for this special love of God. It is unconditional and free as real love always is.

The correct response to that question, *Why me?* is not, Because I did this or that. The correct answer is simply Alleluia. The special love of God is not meant to fuel our pride, but our praise. It awakens in our hearts humble gratitude, the gratitude of those who cannot for the life of them imagine why God should love them, but rejoice in the assurance that he does.

God's Sovereign Majesty (Ps. 148)

The logic of Psalm 148 is first to celebrate the heavens and the earth, and then to praise the Lord because he is over both of them (vv. 1, 7, 13). The psalmist explores just about every area of human knowledge to catalogue the potential members of his cosmic congregation.

He begins in the field of *cosmology:* angels, stars, and waters above the skies (vv. 2–4). Then when he has satisfied himself that he has exhausted the celestial realm, he turns to the terrestrial. *Marine biology:* great sea creatures and all ocean depths. *Meteorology:* lightning and hail, snow and clouds, stormy winds that do his bidding. *Geomorphology* and *dendrology:* mountains and hills, fruit trees and all cedars. *Zoology* and *ornithology:* wild animals, cattle, small creatures, and flying birds. And to cap it all, *political geography*, *sociology,* and *anthropology:* kings of the earth, all nations, princes and rulers, young men and maidens, old men and children. There really can't have been many unthumbed articles left in his encyclopedia. He binds them all together with another "ology," *doxology:* "Let them praise the name of the LORD, for his name alone is exalted; his splendor is above the earth and the heavens."

The purpose of this long excursus on celestial and terrestrial phenomena is to drive home to the worshiping people of God how uniquely

Psalm 148

[1] Praise the LORD.

Praise the LORD from the heavens,
   praise him in the heights above.
[2] Praise him, all his angels,
   praise him, all his heavenly hosts.
[3] Praise him, sun and moon,
   praise him, all you shining stars.
[4] Praise him, you highest heavens
   and you waters above the skies.
[5] Let them praise the name of the LORD,
   for he commanded and they were
      created.
[6] He set them in place for ever and ever;
   he gave a decree that will never pass
      away.

[7] Praise the LORD from the earth,
   you great sea creatures and all ocean
      depths,
[8] lightning and hail, snow and clouds,
   stormy winds that do his bidding,
[9] you mountains and all hills,
   fruit trees and all cedars,
[10] wild animals and all cattle,
   small creatures and flying birds,
[11] kings of the earth and all nations,
   you princes and all rulers on earth,
[12] young men and maidens,
   old men and children.

[13] Let them praise the name of the
      LORD,
   for his name alone is exalted;
   his splendor is above the earth and the
      heavens.
[14] He has raised up for his people a horn,
   the praise of all his saints,
   of Israel, the people close to his heart.

Praise the LORD.

great their God is. There is nobody and nothing in this entire cosmos that does not owe him worship. This was important for the people of God; pagans in the ancient world often worshiped angels and stars. They often attributed the variety of natural phenomena in the world around them to demons and spirits, resident in trees and rivers. Of course, pagans of the modern world are a bit more sophisticated than that. They do not worship angels or stars; they worship science and technology. They attribute the variety of phenomena in nature to impersonal laws resident in protons and neutrons and electrons. But I suspect it is questionable which sort of pagan is actually the more naive. The psalmist would have both learn the folly of their superstitions. It is the Lord who set the stars in heaven; it is the Lord who controls the winds of the earth. His name alone is exalted. There is no other God. That is why the universe is ordered in the remarkably singular and integrated way it is. That is why it holds together as a unity.

And that is why we must be worshipers. There can be no praise or worship unless we have a sense of the felt majesty of God. The trouble with many modern people is that we have small views of God and large views of humanity. Great is man and greatly to be praised, sing the prophets of our contemporary humanism.

A few years back, an educational magazine did a survey of children's ideas of God. It was very revealing: "God is very kind and good and handsome"; "I think he has a white coat and black hair"; "I like God because he puts ideas into my head when I am in trouble with my sums"; "I think God is a very nice man because he is kind to everybody"; "I think God is like us." Unsophisticated as children's minds are, one thing is conspicuous by its absence in their observations. There is no sense of the majesty of God; it has fallen out of the popular imagination of twentieth century human beings. Not for us the traumatic vision of Isaiah, the throne high and lifted up; not for us the prostration of John before the radiant glory of a face like the sun, shining in his strength; not for us the burning bush or the cloudy pillar; not for us Job with his hands clasped to his mouth, speechless in self-loathing that he had been impudent enough to even speak the name of God. No, God is our heavenly Buddy; we favor him with our friendships and patronize him with our prayers. He is a great source of comfort to us, but never, never a source of fear. He makes us feel warm and cozy, but he never makes us feel awe and wonder. He is large enough for our convenience, but small enough for our pocket.

A. W. Tozer said that worship is the missing jewel of the church today, and this is the reason. Only when we realize that the power and intelligence of God encompasses the entire universe, that he holds galaxies in the palms of his hands, will we worship him. There are no mysteries for him: from the vast dimensions of the cosmos to the particle physics of the atom; from the microbiology of the living cell to the psychology of the human brain, he knows it all. His splendor is over the earth and the heavens. He is the uncontested sovereign of the universe, and unless we know that's what he is; unless we have allowed the Bible to teach us that's what he is; unless we have abandoned our small ideas of God and embraced this majestic, gigantic idea of God, we will never praise him. For he will never be worth praising.

How big is your God? Maybe one of the most helpful things any of us can do, if we want to get somewhere near what the Bible means by worship and praise, is to try to remember the most startling, the most admirable, the most spectacular, the most impressive experience we have ever had. I remember the first and only time I looked into the Grand Canyon. Unbelievable grandeur! Maybe you have had an experience like that. Maybe for some of us it was the first time we looked in a microscope and saw all that amazing traffic of the living cell. Maybe for some of us it was a mathematical equation that provoked a sense of amazement and shock and admiration. Or maybe for some of us it was reading a great novel that moved us dramatically to the depths of our being. If we can identify such an experience and multiply it up by a factor of a million, then maybe we are getting near what it means to stand in the presence of a God who is as great as the Bible says he is. Then maybe we are getting somewhere close to what it means to praise and worship. You can't worship a small God.

God's Moral Victory over Evil (Ps. 149)

The tambourine and the harp were traditional instruments, used in triumphal marches after success in battle. There is little doubt that Psalm

---

Psalm 149

¹Praise the LORD.

Sing to the LORD a new song,
 his praise in the assembly of the saints.

²Let Israel rejoice in their Maker;
 let the people of Zion be glad in their
  King.
³Let them praise his name with dancing
 and make music to him with tambourine and harp.
⁴For the LORD takes delight in his people;
 he crowns the humble with salvation.
⁵Let the saints rejoice in this honor

and sing for joy on their beds.

⁶May the praise of God be in their mouths
 and a double-edged sword in their hands,
⁷to inflict vengeance on the nations
 and punishment on the peoples,
⁸to bind their kings with fetters,
 their nobles with shackles of iron,
⁹to carry out the sentence written against them.
 This is the glory of all his saints.

Praise the LORD.

149 is modeled on the victory songs that would be composed afresh to commemorate such occasions. That is why it begins, "Sing to the LORD a new song" (v. 1).

The context isn't difficult to reconstruct. The people of God had been in danger, but their king had led them against their enemies, and God had delivered them, militarily inadequate though they were. So they are able to say that the Lord takes delight in his people (v. 4); he crowns the humble with salvation, that is, deliverance. Now his people, rather like those street crowds on V-E Day, are over the moon with relief and jubilation.

Do they "sing on their beds" because they are so excited they can't sleep at night? Or does it refer to the peace and security that they enjoy now, able to sleep safely in their beds where before they had to keep watch? Or is it, as some suggest, a reference to the couches they recline on as they share their festal meal together? One thing is sure, a great victory has been won, and where there is a winner there is always a loser. So we read:

> May the praise of God be in their mouths
> > and a double-edged sword in their hands,
> to inflict vengeance on the nations
> > and punishment on the peoples (149:6–7).

This is a side of God's character which many protest to find unacceptable or even sub-Christian. But there is no question that the Bible generally sees God's victory over evil and the triumphal vindication of his people as very much a source of inspiration for praise, worship, and gratitude. Winning a battle in the Old Testament was something to be glad about, and that is true not just of the Old Testament, but in a way it is true of the New Testament as well. The nature of battle has changed, that's all. The church of Jesus Christ is no longer a political state threatened by hostile nations; she is a spiritual people. Therefore her foes, as the apostle Paul tells us, are spiritual forces of wickedness. The double-edged sword in her hand is the Word of God, and the battleground where she must fight is that of secular ideology and philosophy.

But make no mistake about it, God's war against evil is a real one, and there will be casualties. There will be those who, at the end of the day, come under divine judgment because they have fought on the wrong side. The Bible is under no illusions about this. John, in the Book of Revelation, is not embarrassed to portray Jesus Christ himself as a warrior general, mounted on a white steed, going into battle at the head of his church. Nor is John ashamed when the saints in glory, on hearing of the victory of the Messiah, burst into a song of triumph, just like this psalm: "Hallelujah! Salvation and glory and power belong to our God. . . . He has avenged on her the blood of his servants. . . . The smoke from her goes up for ever and ever" (Rev. 19:1–3).

Unpalatable as it is to the modern mind, the Bible insists that God is glorified in judgment. Divine retribution is not some skeleton in God's theological cupboard that everybody in heaven is too embarrassed to talk about. On the contrary, heaven praises God for hell. For heaven knows there can be no heaven without it. If you want a world of peace and justice there can be no pact with unrighteousness, no appeasement of the wicked, no Munich Agreement with the devil. Evil must be conquered and eternally destroyed or else the people of God will go on weeping and suffering for all eternity. God will not have it.

So Alleluia is not in the Bible just a word of faith, or gratitude, or admiration; it is also a word of triumph; it is a word of victory. Evil may be intimidating, but its days are numbered. God has uttered his sentence against it. And, says the psalmist, that sentence will be executed (v. 9).

A Final Celebration of Praise (Ps. 150)

More than any other psalm in these five, Psalm 150 comes closest to being a vehicle for simply elevating the emotions. You can almost hear the crescendo, as each section of the temple orchestra joins in the crashing final chorus of praise in verses 3–5. First the brass, "the sounding trumpet"; then the strings, "the harp and the lyre"; then the percussion, "the tambourine and the clashing cymbal." Some from a conservative tradition may demand, Where is the reverence in all this? Worship should surely be something quiet, grave, respectful.

Or should it? Sometimes it can be like that, but here the saints of God are celebrating. There is a victory that has been won. Here is a God who, unlike the kings of the earth, can be depended upon to vindicate the weak. In his special love for his people, he has stepped down

173

> # Psalm 150
>
> [1]Praise the LORD.
>
> Praise God in his sanctuary;
>   praise him in his mighty heavens.
> [2]Praise him for his acts of power;
>   praise him for his surpassing greatness.
> [3]Praise him with the sounding of the
>   trumpet,
> praise him with the harp and lyre,
> [4]praise him with tambourine and dancing,
>   praise him with the strings and flute,
> [5]praise him with the clash of cymbals,
>   praise him with resounding cymbals.
>
> [6]Let everything that has breath praise
>   the LORD.
>
> Praise the LORD.

from his awesome majesty in heaven and by the strength of his arm, he has delivered them, routing the forces of evil, and reopening the doors of paradise to them. You can't praise a God like that with your lips close together. One thing John is sure about in the Book of Revelation is that heaven is full of music. Everywhere you look, people are singing or playing musical instruments. For heaven is a place of joy, a place to celebrate who this God is and what he has done.

Yet it is important to note that the psalmist will not allow his Alleluias to be vehicles of mere emotionalism:

> Praise him for his acts of power;
>   praise him for his surpassing greatness (150:2).

You must have *reasons* to praise this God. And the people of God have reasons.

For all its brevity, this psalm has something to teach us about the controversial issue of music in the church. There are some who want to argue that certain instruments are biblical and others are not; certain styles of music are reverent and others are not. In the light of Psalm 150 it is difficult to draw lines like that. Music is culturally conditioned; what feels right as an appropriate expression of joy and celebration differs from people to people. We must beware of inventing spurious theological arguments to sanctify our particular musical taste and to impose a ban upon all others. History is not kind to those who thought they knew the only biblical way to worship God. The church has, generally speaking, given up on them after a few years, and decided they were wrong.

174

There is only one thing you can say about the use of music in worship. It is really enshrined in those opening and closing words: "Praise the LORD." If music is to be praise and worship, it must be God-directed. It simply won't do to come and do my own musical thing in church and call that praise. Many a choir item, many a special number, many an organ voluntary, if the true motivations of hearts were laid bare, would be found to be a human-directed, human-glorifying thing. We may want to dignify it with the title worship or praise, but God does not.

This is a particular hazard for the young who are trying to express their love for God in musically contemporary ways. All too often the pop singer, the beat guitarist, and the jazz drummer of today are idols. And Christian groups can be infected with the same kind of worldly pride. The applause and the admiration of others can quickly become an intoxicating drug that mars those who want to stand up and sing for Jesus. Worship in music has to begin and end with Alleluia, praise the Lord. For that reason, it is not the professionalism of the performance that counts, though it is right to do our best; it is not the genius of the composition or the profundity of the words that matters, because if that were the case the tambourine player would be a bit limited. No, it is the intended audience that counts; it is the One whom we are intending to glorify in what we are doing. That is what determines whether music is real music in praise of God or not.

I referred earlier to A. W. Tozer's comment that worship was the missing jewel in the modern church. I fear many are looking in the wrong direction to find that elusive gem. Some look in the direction of meditation; some look in the direction of liturgy; some look in the direction of emotionalism; some look in the direction of music or dance. It is not that any of these things are wrong in themselves, but none of them provides the key to real worship. The focus of true worship is *truth:* the truth about *God,* who he is, and what he has done. Praise him for his acts of power. Praise him for his surpassing greatness. That's what fires the word of praise. If you know God today, this faithful, loving, majestic, victorious God; if you know him firsthand, you can be a worshiper. Alleluia will come as naturally to your lips as a smile to a baby's face.

It is perhaps interesting that in placing this great paean of praise at its end, the Book of Psalms differs from most modern hymnbooks.

Invariably, our hymnals are compiled with hymns of praise at the beginning and then peter out at the end in the indices, the acknowledgments, and the national anthem. Not so the Psalter. Many of its earliest numbers emerge out of struggle and conflict, doubt and fear. It reserves its greatest chorus of praise for the end. Maybe that's significant, for in the Bible, although worship is where the people of God end up, it is not necessarily where they begin. Maybe there was a time in your life when you didn't feel like praising God. To have taken the word Alleluia to your lips then would have been a sham and a hypocrisy. Take encouragement from the psalms. It will not always be so.

Even if there was a time when we didn't praise God; even if we didn't feel like praising God when we woke up today, we ought to feel like praising him now because we have learned things from his Word about him. If you find worship hard, if you find emotional engagement with hymns and choruses difficult, if you find yourself embarrassed by the exuberance others display when they are moved in worship, my advice to you is quite simple: stop looking at others. Stop looking at Brother X who bounces the hymnbook when he sings, and Sister Y who insists on raising her hands when she prays, and stop looking inside yourself as if contemplating your navel were somehow going to arouse spiritual emotion in you.

If you want to become a worshiper, focus your mind on God. Become preoccupied with him: his unchanging character, you can depend upon it; his special love, which he has for you in particular; his sovereign majesty, which dazzles the cosmos; his triumphal victory, which will eliminate evil and rebuild the paradise we lost so many years ago. Focus your mind upon him. Then you will find Alleluia rising to your lips as it rose to the psalmist's, and you will realize that whatever your song of experience was in the past, it can finish with Alleluia, the song of praise.